.

This Is Not the Life I Ordered

50 Ways to keep
your head above water
when life keeps
dragging you down

Deborah Collins Stephens · Jackie Speier
Jan Yanehiro · Michealene Cristini Risley

MJF BOOKS
NEW YORK

Published by MJF Books
Fine Communications
322 Eighth Avenue
New York, NY 10001

This Is Not the Life I Ordered
LC Control Number: 2015959284
ISBN 978-1-60671-344-0

Illustrations © 2009 by John Grimes

The phrase "Courage doesn't always roar" was coined by Mary Anne Radmacher.
Used with permission.

This edition is published by MJF Books in arrangement with Red Wheel/Weiser, LLC.

Printed in the United States of America.

MJF Books and the MJF colophon are trademarks of Fine Creative Media, Inc.

QF   10   9   8   7   6   5   4   3   2   1

If one woman sees another woman as successful, that woman will never fail, never feel alone. . . .
—Florence Scovel Shinn, writer (1871–1940)

Contents

Chapter Four: Understanding Money and a Woman's Worth

Chapter Five: Learning to Live with Change

Chapter Six: Reinventing Yourself

Chapter Seven: Real Women Ask for Help!

Chapter Eight: Facing Naysayers

Chapter Nine: Rebuilding Dreams

Acknowledgments

We are indebted to the many women who shared their stories with us. Their contributions have made for a good book, but more important, they have enriched our lives in ways that will stay with us forever. In particular: Gerry Laybourne, Cynthia Modders, Margaret Loesch, Kiran Bedi, Sarah Little Turnbull, Suki Forbes Bigham, Saranne Rothberg, Denise Garibaldi, Vornida Seng, Lisa Bentley, Kristi Yamaguchi, Mimi Silbert, Rose Guilbault, Kathleen Wentworth, Nancy Pedot, Dr. Judith Orloff, Susie Tompkins Buell, Sam Horn, Cindy Solomon, Peggy Klaus, Kathryn Tunstall, Radha Basu, Jane Williams, Emile Goldman, Barbara Stanny, Linda Ellerbee, Amy Tan, Marta McGinnis Blodgett, Francine Ward, Laurel Burch, Rita Moreno, and Marcia Wieder. Thank you for being wise and inspirational women from whom we can all learn.

We acknowledge our families for their patience and understanding as we spent time away from them while writing. To Mike Stephens, Eric Risley, Barry Dennis, and Robert Eves, thank you for believing in this project and us—even if it did take more years than anyone imagined! To our children, Lily and Aaron Stephens; Dillon, Christopher, and Austin Risley; Stephanie and Jackson Sierra; Jenna, J.B. and Jaclyn Zimmerman; Christopher and Meredith Eves: thank you for being the loves of our lives!

To our close friends and family members Doris Mason, Gary Heil, Nancy Parrish, Margo Rosen, Christine Krolik, Nancy and Fred Speier, Eric and Laurel Speier, Katy Lawson, Stacy Dwellcy, Erin Ryan, Elise Thurau, Tracy Fairchild, Sheryl Young, Helen Raiser, Deborah Strobin, Helen Mendel, Christine Franco, Margaret Lyon, Jennifer Raiser, Kathleen Alioto, Adrienne Tissier, Sharon Kime, Judy Swanson, Cynthia Schuman, Barbara Kaplan, Betty Dennis, Richard Steffen, Brian Perkins, Laura Wilkinson Zimmerman, Ann and Al

Zimmerman, Debby Jones, Elaine Petrocelli, Bonnie Engel, Gwenda Williams, David Whitehead, Keiko Smith, Renee Ortiz, Linda Uyehara, Cindy Martin, Derick Yanehiro, Beatrice Yanehiro, Chrissie Kremer, Donna Garrison, and Patricia Wynne.

We also owe a debt of gratitude to Anne Robinson Kasten and Nancy Olsen, who were original members of our kitchen table group. Their inspiration and wisdom continue with us.

Ruth Stergiou of Planning Dynamics and the Professional and Business Women's Conference of California has been a wonderful supporter, always bringing us back each year to speak at the largest gathering of professional women in the west. Thank you, Ruth, for believing in us.

Sam Horn, author, coach, and chief cheerleader, your remarkable touches made all the difference to our manuscript. Jillian Manus, super agent, who helped us through the years and who gave us the metaphor "survive and thrive" that described our lives in perfect fashion. Julia Van Horn, designer extraordinaire who has been with us from the beginning when we pursued our self-publishing route. To Jan Johnson and her terrific team at Conari Press and Red Wheel/ Weiser who encouraged us, inspired us, and greatly improved our manuscript. We thank you.

Finally, John Grimes *(www.grimescartoons.com)*, the funniest man we know, you read every word of our manuscript and delivered the illustrations that make women laugh every time!

Introduction to the Paperback Edition

Hope Is a Strategy

Thousands of books sold, hundreds of interviews completed, numerous speeches given, and garnering enough reviews, personal letters of encouragement, shared stories and precious new women friends, we begin with a **very big thank you.** What started around a kitchen table over a decade ago, with nothing more than a collective goal of re-inventing ourselves in the midst of some pretty bad life circumstances, has resulted in a dream come true. It was a dream to write a book that would give hope, inspiration, encouragement and lessons for any woman, anywhere, anytime, at any age. It was our intent to help women believe that obstacles could be overcome and lives could be re-built.

The paperback version of *This Is Not the Life I Ordered* enters a world that feels most days like a runaway train. Headlines read and television anchors scream that we have entered the worst financial crisis since the Great Depression. Truly it is a time that few of us saw coming and none of us ordered. It is also a time to believe that hope for a brighter tomorrow is not only a necessary strategy but a healthy and powerful way to live with the anxiety and fear that seems to be piercing the hearts of women everywhere. In these historic, emotional, and uncertain days, this book offers 50 ways to keep your head above water when life keeps dragging you down. It is a message for *today*.

There is no better time than now to form your own kitchen table group—a place where women come together to develop strategies, tactics, ideas, and avenues of opportunity. This book gives you a road-map for creating your own group and a framework for sparking your motivation. Our mission is to fill you with enthusiasm and possibility even as world circumstances threaten to deplete you.

We Pushed the Reset Button!

Since the publication of the book, we four authors have undergone tremendous personal and professional changes. Jan Yanehiro says, "My divorce should be final in the next couple of months. So by the time this book comes out, I hope to be single. Single . . . and living in an 1880 Victorian in San Francisco and loving city life!

"My children are in all parts of the country. Jaclyn Zimmerman works in Washington DC for Congresswoman Mazie Hirono from Hawaii; Jenna Zimmerman works at the Food Network in New York City, and my son J.B. Zimmerman is a junior at the University of Arizona in Tucson. And I choose to remain close to all my stepchildren, Laura Wilkinson and Meredith and Christopher Eves.

"Divorce has been unbelievably painful, so the next book I would like to write will be 'This Is Not the Husband I Ordered.' But with change comes new opportunity—and a great one landed in my lap: To start a brand new School of Multimedia Communications for the Academy of Art University in San Francisco. When I accepted the directorship, I said to Elisa Stephens, the president of the University, 'You know, I'm old and I'm bossy . . . and I can make this happen for you!' In two months, we had built a studio, hired faculty and designed a 4-year degree program as well as a master's program. It's amazing how students can make you feel young and inspire you to learn with them about re-inventing yourself! Recently, Jen Siebel Newsom (wife of the mayor of San Francisco) and I debuted a new show, *Giving 5 with Jan and Jen* on KPIX TV in San Francisco. We interview stars like an Olympic gold medalist, athletes, philanthropists, and students about how they are giving back to their neighborhoods, to communities, to the world. Life is full. And if I ever need a safety net, my girlfriends are there. And I am grateful."

Jackie Speier lost her election for Lt. Governor of California by less than three points and ended her term as a state senator. Taking a job in a law firm with a dogged determination to continue in public service but no clear path for doing so, Jackie had a "desire versus destiny" moment. She ended up running for the 12th Congressional seat in the House of Representatives, the same seat that her late mentor Congressman Leo Ryan held. Jackie won by 79% of the vote 1-½ years later in an unexpected turn of events. "Always expect the unexpected or at least be prepared," Jackie says.

In her first official act as congresswoman, Speier gave a speech on the House floor in which she condemned the war in Iraq and requested withdrawal of our troops. She was roundly booed by her Republican colleagues, and one member even walked out in protest. On the first day on the job, the world was introduced to the Jackie we know and love—a courageous and caring representative of those she serves. Her children continue to flourish. Stephanie is a freshman in high school and Jackson is a junior at Stanford University.

Michealene took a trip to Africa and it wasn't a vacation. She was in search of a story on the terrible plight of young women and children in Zimbabwe. Arrested and interrogated by Zimbabwean officials, Michealene and her crew were thrown out of the country. In the months that followed, Michealene continued her work as a human rights activist. She speaks out on issues affecting women and children and has addressed audiences at The United Nations, Amnesty International, Google, and Stanford's Entrepreneurial Thought Leaders lecture series.

In 2008, her most recent directing project is *Tapestries of Hope*, a project designed to foster awareness of the rape and abuse of infants and children in Zimbabwe to "cure" AIDS. She blogs frequently for the *Huffington Post*, and recently won the New Communications Review's Award of Excellence. With her husband Eric, Michealene found and sold their dream house, and then moved into the guest house! Together with their children Christopher, Austin, and Dillon, they have realized that home is truly where the heart is.

Deborah and her family made a life-changing decision to sell their home of 25 years in the San Francisco Bay Area and move to the small Midwestern town of Bloomington, Indiana. She wanted to be nearer to her family. "It was a decision based only upon what we value, and those values trumped issues of culture, job opportunities, long-standing friendships and weather." It's been two years and although she's weathered some significant ups and downs, it has certainly been worth it. She's preparing for the next act, the next chapter—some days it seems clear, and other days she can hardly find the roadmap. However, she knows deep inside that she is exactly where she needs to be. Her children continue to prosper. Lily is a junior in high school and Aaron is a senior at Indiana University. Mike continues as an everyday hero in fighting against his illness.

Thank you for buying our book, for supporting us and encouraging us. May you climb into a new life and achieve your dreams. Know that we will be cheering you on.

Deborah Collins Stephens
Michealene Cristini Risley
Jackie Speier
Jan Yanehiro

preface

Slightly Less Than Worst-Case Scenarios

Whether one is twenty, forty, or sixty; whether one has succeeded, failed, or just muddled along; whether yesterday was full of sun or storm, or one of those dull days with no weather at all, life begins again each morning in the heart of a woman.

—Leigh Mitchell Hodges, poet (1876–1954)

We are simply four women whom destiny threw together more than a decade ago. Collectively, we have experienced the extreme joys and deep sorrows that life offers up. From mundane moments to the dramatic and surreal, we have a history of six marriages, ten children, four stepchildren, six dogs, two miscarriages, two cats, twelve koi fish, a failed adoption, widowhood, and foster parenthood. We have built companies, lost companies, and sold companies. One of us was shot and left for dead on a tarmac in South America, and two of us have lived through the deaths of spouses.

We're raising babies and teenagers and are still alive to talk about it. We've had our hearts broken by affairs and mended through our friendships. We've known celebrity and loneliness along with self-doubt and near financial ruin. We've been caregivers to those who faced terminal illnesses and friends to those who lost loved ones.

We grew up in less-than-wealthy families, where living paycheck to paycheck was the norm. We've known more wealth than our parents could ever imagine, and we've lost more money than they ever made! Forced to be creative, we have raised families on bare budgets and at times have been the sole breadwinners and bakers when our spouses were unemployed, seriously ill, or dying.

We have won and lost elections and Emmys, starred on television, written books, and graced the covers of magazines. In our fast-paced careers, we've often been the only woman at the table in deals made Silicon Valley style. We have taken risks that have bet the company, bet the election, and—in some cases—bet the house!

(A COLLECTION OF MISFORTUNATE EVENTS)

When Bad Things Happen to Smart Women

There are two ways of meeting difficulties: you alter the difficulties or you alter yourself meeting them.

—*Phyllis Bottome, English writer (1884—1963)*

A reporter once jokingly referred to our collection of misfortunate events as the female version of the book of Job, almost expecting a hoard of locusts ready to descend in our midst at any moment! Yet, we do not view our lives with sadness or remorse. We see them as gifts, filled with events that have helped us develop a razor-sharp sense of what counts and what simply doesn't. Time and again, we have learned to reinvent ourselves. The process of reinvention, we've learned, is best managed with humor, friendship, optimism, and a long-lasting high-beam flashlight to see the light at the end of every tunnel.

Meeting monthly, we've shared our lives with one another and encouraged one another. Our kitchen table conversations were always therapeutic. Inspiring and supportive, our conversations gave us hope and inner strength. We knew that together, as friends, we would never walk alone in our life's journey. Yet, as individuals, we could not be more different. We share a common ground, though: the transitions we've faced as women. All women will face such transitions at some point in their lives.

Kitchen Table Friends
It's the friend you call up at four o'clock in the morning that really matters.
— Marlene Dietrich, German actress (1901–1992)

Word spread about our kitchen table conversations. We were asked to speak at the Professional and Business Women's Conference, at the California Governor's Conference, and even by *Inc.* magazine. We titled our talk "Survive and Thrive: Ten Turbo Charged Tips for Women in Transition" and guessed that maybe, if we were lucky, thirty people might show up for the conversation.

Over four hundred women came to our first session, forcing the fire marshals to lock the doors! We told our stories that day. Women lined up to talk with us. They shared their own personal versions of "survive and thrive" lives. Weeks later, we were encouraged to write a book. More conference organizers asked us to speak. We used the idea of writing a book as an excuse to continue our monthly meetings, yet we never wrote a single word.

We Gave Our Group a Name

Expect trouble as an inevitable part of life and repeat to yourself the most comforting words of all: this too shall pass.
—*Ann Landers, newspaper columnist (1918–2002)*

We continued to meet for over a decade before we put one word onto paper for that imaginary book we told everyone we were writing! We talked about losing businesses, losing husbands, and wanting to lose husbands. We talked about building careers, building families, and building on our fragile networking skills. We talked about finding our self-esteem, finding our path, even finding new mates. We talked about taking on challenges, taking risks, and taking a chance on love again. We talked candidly about near financial ruin, actual financial ruin, and avoiding financial ruin. We talked about high moments, low moments, and defining moments. We talked about personal events that had shaped our lives and, in some cases, rocked our lives. We talked about our children, our coworkers, our colleagues, and our sex lives. No topic in our lives was left unexplored!

We encouraged one another through the numerous transitions we were experiencing. We even gave ourselves a name—Women in Transition, "WIT" for short—noting that we would truly need our collective wit to navigate through these tricky times. Interestingly enough, our "meetings" took the form of what we envisioned as an 1800s ladies quilting club in the Wild West. Yet the fabric we brought to our meetings was the fabric of our lives.

We learned an important lesson in our decade-long friendships. We learned that we had been fooled. We had convinced ourselves that if we could manage our schedules, break through the glass ceiling, spend quality time with our families, bring home the bacon (and fry it up in a pan) while bouncing children on our hips and creating warm and loving relationships with our husbands, in-laws, and colleagues, somehow, some way, we would be rewarded with the problem-free lives that had, up until then, eluded us. We were wrong.

Nike for Some, Nine West for Others

I never lose an opportunity of urging a practical beginning, however small, for it is wonderful how often the mustard seed germinates and roots itself to greatness.

—Florence Nightingale, English nurse (1820–1910)

From kitchen conversations to the thousands of conversations we've had with women from all over the world, we learned that the problem-free life we sought was more than an illusion. It had become a myth to which too many women had fallen victim. A woman's life is much more than success, having it all, or the elusive balance we all seek. It is more than seeking perfection or conquering the world (although you might). It is more than gritting your teeth and making it through. It is about surviving and thriving.

For us, surviving and thriving meant reinventing, rebuilding, and realizing that success was never final and failure was never fatal. It meant putting our best foot forward (Nike for some, Nine West for others) no matter what, and walking. Walking forward looking like a pillar of success on the outside while that tiny voice inside reminded us that our teenagers were out of control, our job could end tomorrow, and our spouses, colleagues, and bosses had been untruthful, selfish, unfaithful, or just plain stupid.

Surviving and thriving meant taking what life offered up and looking for the opportunities, the joy, and the compassion in less-than-pleasant or less-than-perfect circumstances. It meant cultivating the collective willpower to move up and move on, or move out, even when the process broke our hearts. It meant recruiting support and building the confidence to trust that when life's legendary curveballs were thrown, we would have the willpower, support, and courage to move forward. The phrase "survive and thrive" became a perfect descriptor of our journeys as friends. Together we would navigate through some tricky times.

So, How's Your Life?
Anybody singing the blues is in a deep pit yelling for help.
— *Mahalia Jackson, gospel singer (1911–1972)*

Our collective lives have been filled with more transitions and life changes than we would have ever thought possible. Transitions are an important part of the fabric of every woman's life. They affect us individually but also have a ripple effect that we witness in our families and communities.

Transitions can build our character and turn us into wise women, or they can leave us feeling depressed and alone. Successful transitions can make us strong—ready to extend a hand to other women who will join us—or they can make us fearful of what lies ahead.

You might be thinking, who are these women and what are their credentials? Well, we are not psychologists (although we have seen a few). We are not self-help experts (although we have read the books). We don't profess to have discovered any ultimate truths. We are simply four women who have banded together and helped each other get through our lives.

Construct a "Wit Kit"

The way I see it, if you want a rainbow, you gotta put up with the rain.
  —Dolly Parton, singer (1946–)

This book is a road map of sorts for life's transitions. It contains the many lessons we've learned on how to maneuver the tidal waves of change that threatened our stability.

Along the way, we have been honored to meet and interview many magnificent women. We've included their stories of challenge, resilience, and triumph. This book is a literary kitchen table, where we invite you to pull up a chair and join us so you don't have to go through life alone. We hope this inspiring circle of women gives you the hope, insight, and inspiration to deal with your own challenges and changes.

We agree with Thomas à Kempis, who said, "The object of education isn't knowledge; it's action." With that in mind, each section in this book ends with suggested action plans and exercises. We call this section the WIT Kit. We hope you'll find the insights we've shared interesting. Even more important, we hope you'll be motivated to take the time to adapt and apply them in your life, where they can produce real-world results.

We know you're busy. We know you're probably running from the minute you wake up to the minute you go to bed. What we've learned, though, is that taking the time to follow up on the recommendations in the WIT Kit has made the difference between merely surviving what life has thrown at us and thriving despite what life has thrown at us.

Some of the suggested steps in the WIT Kit take only a few minutes. Some involve more time and planning. All of them can help. If you feel as though life is dragging you down, these actions can help you keep your head above water. They can help you create a higher quality of life for yourself and your loved ones now, not someday.

Deborah Collins Stephens
Michealene Cristini Risley
Jackie Speier
Jan Yanehiro
San Francisco, California
October 2006

chapter one

Managing Misfortunate Events

1. Convene a gathering of kitchen table friends.

If I had to characterize one quality as the genius of female thought, culture, and action, it would be the connectivity.
— Robin Morgan, writer (1941–)

Find One Safe Place to Tell Your Story
You are the storyteller of your own life and you can create the legend or not.
— Isabel Allende, Chilean-American writer (1942–)

For over ten years, the four of us gathered round a kitchen table and told our stories. We looked forward to our gatherings because we knew that it was the one place in our lives where we would be heard. It was a place where other women would listen intently without judgment. We can state without one ounce of doubt that being able to tell our story to another woman saved our sanity and, in some cases, saved our lives.

We believe that every woman needs to create for herself a safe place where her story can be heard. A place and time convened with women friends who care about her well-being. We know from our own experience that staying connected with each other has made all the difference in our ability to cope with the challenges we've faced over the years. Our first and most important way to keep your head above water when life threatens to drag you down is to convene a gathering of kitchen table friends. Form this group so you have an ongoing source of support.

Think you don't have time for your women friends? We encourage you to think again. If you're thinking, "I don't feel up to doing this right now," that's precisely why you ought to do this. If your energy is low, it's because you're trying to do everything by yourself.

You're running on empty, and you need to fill up your emotional tank with support and input from women who care about you. Kitchen table groups will feed your soul. You can get started today with seven simple steps. Following these steps can help you create a wonderful network of women friends.

Seven Steps for Forming a Kitchen Table Group
A friend walks in when the rest of the world walks out.
—*Anonymous*

1. No matter how bad your life might be right now, plan a get-together with women you admire. They do not need to be famous, rich, or fabulously accomplished. You do not need to know them well; although they do need to be women you respect and who share similar values and priorities—women with integrity who will be willing to listen, encourage others, and be honest.

   Many women feel as isolated as you do. Now is the perfect time to ask that mom who shares car pool duties with you. What about the woman at work with whom you have only a nodding acquaintance but have always felt a spark of connection? Perhaps there's someone on a fundraising committee you've admired in action, someone who always can be counted on to do what she says she's going to do.

2. Pick a meeting place that has comfortable surroundings and that gives you privacy. It could be the corner of a local coffee shop, the back table at a favorite restaurant, or the living room of your home. The kitchen tables in our different homes have worked well for us all these years.

3. You don't have to do anything fancy. Just pick up the phone, send an e-mail, or ask the women in person. Tell them up front that you know they're busy, that the purpose of this meeting is to create a support network that meets regularly where women can talk out what's going on in their lives in a confidential setting. Participants are welcome to talk about their jobs (or lack of a job), their families, their health, and their finances—whatever is on their minds and in their hearts. Give your group a name and commit to meetings (every other week, or at least monthly). In our own group we met monthly but often convened our kitchen table group more often when one of our members was in the midst of a crisis.

4. The first few meetings of your kitchen table group can probably benefit from some sort of structure. In our group meetings, we always begin with some illuminating questions:

   • So, how's your life?
   • How can we help?
   • Who do we know who can help?
   • What are you happy about right now in your life?
   • What is there to laugh about?
   • When we leave here today, what three things are we committing to each other that we will do for ourselves?

5. Do not allow your kitchen table groups to turn into a "pity party." Pity parties rob you of your spirit and do nothing to empower you. The purpose of this gathering is not simply to complain . . . and stop there. Go ahead and get what's bothering you, worrying you, or hurting you off your chest, and then

ask for advice. Brainstorm possible solutions and strategies for the issues you're facing. Have fun, cry, and laugh out loud.

6. Use the WIT Kit found at the end of each part in this book as a focus for your meetings. We purposely created the WIT Kit with exercises that you can work through as a group in your own kitchen table meetings. Discuss the topics and questions among your group.

7. Visit our website *www.thisisnotthelifeiordered.com* for more resources on kitchen table groups. Also, let us know about your group and tell us your stories.

The Stories We've Told

If there is a secret about how to make a woman's circle it is that the women in the circle know each other's personal stories, know about each other's journeys, know what is of consequence, where the challenges and difficulties are that matter . . .

— Jean Shinoda Bolen, M.D., psychiatrist and writer

Our kitchen table group met for over ten years and during that time we told many stories, solved many problems, and mended many broken hearts. We begin by introducing you to our stories and the defining moments that brought us together as lifelong friends.

2. Transcend misfortunate events.

"Surely, things shall get better," she said. I wanted to know just one thing. Who the hell was "Shirley," and why should I believe her?

— Jane Curtin, comedian (1947–   )

Silly Thoughts

Although there may be tragedy in your life, there's always a possibility to triumph. It doesn't matter who you are, where you come from. The ability to triumph begins with you. Always.

— *Oprah Winfrey, television host (1954—   )*

Nightmares. They still invade my sleep twenty-seven years later. The nightmares remind me that life is a precious resource to be used up, enjoyed, lived.

I am Jackie Speier, and my nightmares take me back to a fateful day in November nearly three decades ago.

I was twenty-eight at the time, getting ready to purchase my first home. As a single professional woman, legislative counsel to a U.S. congressman, I had it all. But I had a strong premonition that the trip I was arranging to South America could be one from which I might not return. "Silly thoughts," my friend Katy assured me. "After all, you will be traveling with the press corps and a U.S. congressman. What could possibly happen?"

Holed up in a congressional office for hours at a time, I was reading State Department briefings on a religious community created by the Reverend Jim Jones. We were investigating numerous allegations from relatives and friends that their family members were being held against their will in a jungle hideaway known as the People's Temple. As we reviewed taped interviews with defectors, I had an ominous feeling—a feeling I could not put out of my mind. One former member had told us that people were being forced to act out suicides in an exercise Jim Jones called "The White Night."

Congressman Leo Ryan, my boss, had heard enough. He decided to see for himself, firsthand, the plight of these U.S. citizens in Guyana, South America. Even after the CIA and the State Department cleared the trip for safety, I still had doubts.

Conversations in a Jungle

I postpone death by living, by suffering, by error, by risking, by loving.
    —*Anaïs Nin, French writer (1903–1977)*

Flying into Guyana's capital, Georgetown, we changed planes and continued on to Port Kaituma—a remote airstrip deep inside the South American jungle. Several convoy trucks drove us to the Jonestown encampment. We entered a clearing in the jungle, where I saw an outdoor amphitheatre surrounded by small cabins. You couldn't help but be impressed by the settlement. In less than two years, a community had been carved out. During our first and only night at the People's Temple, the members entertained us with music and singing. I remember looking into the eyes of Jim Jones. I saw madness there. He was no longer the charismatic leader who had lured more than 900 people to a remote commune in the jungle; he was a man possessed.

The congressman and I randomly selected people to interview to determine whether they were being held against their will. We hand-delivered letters to those whose families back home were worried. Many of the individuals were young—eighteen or nineteen years old—while others were senior citizens. One by one, they told us that they loved living in the People's Temple. It was almost as though they had been coached to answer my questions. As the night drew to a close, NBC news correspondent Don Harris walked off alone to smoke a cigarette. In the darkness, two people approached him and put notes into his hand. The correspondent gave the notes to Congressman Ryan and me. I held in my hands evidence of what I had sensed all along: people were indeed being held against their will in the jungles of South America.

Morning broke, and I interviewed the two people who had sent notes saying they wanted to leave. Word of the opportunity to leave had gotten out. More people started coming forward, stating they too wished to depart. Suddenly a couple of men with guns appeared. Chaos ensued as more people approached us, wanting to leave. Jim Jones started ranting and screaming. Larry Layton, one of Jones's closest assistants, said, "Don't get the wrong idea. We are all very happy here. You see the beauty of this special place." One hour later, Larry Layton had become one of the defectors, asking to escape the jungle compound.

3. When left on the tarmac, begin to walk.

Through experience of trial and suffering can the soul be strengthened, vision cleared, ambition inspired, and fight restored.
—— *Helen Keller, writer (1880–1968)*

Pretending to Die
The world is round and the place which may seem like the end may also be only the beginning.
—— *Ivy Baker Priest, former U.S. Secretary of the Treasury (1905–1975)*

People were screaming and crying in the jungle compound. The tiny commune had become emotionally charged. Parents were in a tug-of-war with their children, one parent wanting to go and the other wanting to stay. So many had decided to escape the People's Temple that we had to order another plane.

We left for the airstrip. Dressed in an oversized yellow poncho, Larry Layton was eager to board the cargo plane. I distrusted him and asked that he be searched before boarding. A journalist patted him down but did not find the gun Layton had hidden under his poncho. Thinking back, I now realize we were helpless. Here we were—a congressman, congressional aides, journalists, and cameramen—not one among us a police officer or military escort. We had nothing to protect us other than the imagined shield of infallibility of a U.S. congressman and members of the U.S. press corps.

Suddenly we heard a scream. Seconds later, I heard an unfamiliar noise. I saw people running into the bushes and realized that the noise was gunshot. I dropped to the ground and curled up around a wheel of the plane, pretending to be dead. I heard footsteps. I felt my body twitch as someone pumped bullets into me at point blank range. I was shot five times.

The gunmen continued to walk around the tarmac, shooting innocent people. Soon it was quiet. I opened my eyes and looked down at my body. It was ravaged. A bone was sticking out of my arm, and blood was everywhere. I remember thinking, "My God, I am twenty-eight years old and I am about to die." I yelled out for Congressman Ryan, calling his name several times. There was no answer.

The plane's engine was still revving, and I thought that if I could just get to the cargo hatch, I could escape this place. I crawled toward the opening, dragging my body as close as I could to the baggage compartment. A reporter from the *Washington Post* picked me up and put me into the cargo hold. I remember saying to him, "Could you give me something to stop my bleeding?" He gave me his shirt. I was losing so much blood that the shirt was soaked in seconds.

The plane was filled with bullet holes, and we soon realized this would not be our flight out of this hell on earth. Someone pulled me out of the plane and placed me back on the airstrip. Accidentally, they had laid my head upon an anthill, and ants started crawling all over me. Lying next to me was a reporter's tape recorder. I taped a last message to my parents and brother. I told them that I loved them.

Supposedly, the Guyanese Army was going to secure the airstrip and rescue us, so I held on tightly to the belief that the army would come. It grew dark, and we continued to wait. Although I was in excruciating pain, I clung to life.

In the middle of the night, word had gotten back to us that there had been a mass suicide at the People's Temple. At one o'clock the next day, twenty hours after the shootings, the Guyanese Air Force arrived. Their arrival coincided with a message to the world that more than 900 people, including a U.S. congressman and members of his delegation, were dead. The headlines called it the worst mass suicide in history. To this day, I still refer to the events at Jonestown as a mass murder.

Three Minutes from Death

Sometimes it takes years to really grasp what has happened to your life.
— *Wilma Rudolph, Olympic gold medal winner (1940–1994)*

The Guyanese Air Force transported the survivors to a waiting U.S. Air Force Medivac plane in Georgetown. Etched in my memory is how I felt that very moment—as though someone had wrapped me in the American flag. I was so grateful.

Loaded with survivors, the Air Force plane set off for the United States. As we taxied down the runway, I recall glancing down at my body. It seemed so surreal, as though the mangled lump of flesh belonged to someone other than me. Months later, I was told that the medical technician who had tended to me during the flight had said that I was three minutes from death.

We finally arrived at Andrews Air Force Base, where I was immediately taken into surgery. I had developed gangrene, and surgeons debated whether to amputate my leg. After four hours of surgery, the nurse wheeled me out of the surgical ward, and there stood my mother, who had traveled from San Francisco to meet me. They told my mother that they needed to transfer me to the Baltimore Shock/ Trauma Center to attempt to stem the spread of gangrene. I begged my mother and the doctors to please take me by ambulance, fearing I would die on another plane flight.

The shock/trauma center was lit with incredibly bright lights. Numerous IVs were hooked up to me. I remember asking the nurse, "How many calories are in all that stuff flowing into my body?"

"Three thousand," she replied.

I said, "Oh, my God, I am going to get so fat!" Interesting, isn't it, how we can lose perspective in the middle of trauma?

After yet another surgery, I was returned to my hospital room. The surgeons had repaired my body, but my hair was still matted with dried blood, Guyanese dirt, and dead ants. In an act of love I will never forget, my brother tenderly washed my hair.

The doctors remained very concerned about the gangrene in my wounds. In a last-ditch effort, they began a series of hyperbaric treatments that required me to be placed into a chamber filled with antibacterial microbes and oxygen. The chamber resembled an iron lung. Each time they removed me from the chamber, I vomited violently. Unfortunately, they had to repeat this process several times over the next few days.

Confident they had gotten rid of the gangrene, they transferred me back to Arlington Hospital. I was also placed under twenty-four-hour protection, with U.S. Marshalls posted outside my door, because threats had been made against my life. Some individuals associated with the People's Temple blamed our congressional investigation for the mass deaths in Guyana and wanted to retaliate.

One Step Forward, One Day at a Time

Challenges make you discover things about yourself that you never really knew. They're what make the instrument stretch—what make you go beyond the norm.

——*Cicely Tyson, actress (1933–)*

The surgeons performed skin grafts on my legs. The gunshots had blown apart my right arm, and a steel dowel had been inserted to hold together what remained. The radial nerve in my arm was damaged, and I could not use my fingers or lift my arm. The first time they tried to get me on my feet to walk, I fainted. Hospitalized for nearly two months and having endured ten surgeries, I was finally discharged and was able to fly back to San Francisco.

The days ahead were a flurry of interviews about the Jonestown massacre. I was not allowed to stay in my home because of the death threats, so I lived with a friend. I still carried two bullets in my body, which the doctors had deemed too risky to remove. I never appeared in public without layers of clothes to cover what I had begun to believe was my hideous, disfigured body. In the following years, I would endure months of physical therapy to regain the use of my arm.

I was twenty-eight, a single woman who could hardly feed herself and whose body was maimed and scarred. One day I realized that if I was going to get over this, if I was ever going to go forward, I had to figure out a way not to wallow in self-pity.

The exact moment I came to terms with what had happened in Guyana occurred years later, on a crowded beach in Hawaii. The disfigured body I walked in was mine. The joy I felt at just being alive had become greater than my insecurities. I had come to realize that a person's body was irrelevant in the big picture of life, physical beauty a shallow concern. I was disabled, but I did not believe that a dis-

ability of any kind prevented me from living a full and wonderful life.
If anything, my disfigurement had opened my eyes to the bias often
harbored toward those who are different.

I put on a bathing suit that day and walked across the Hawaiian
beach as people stared at the remnant scars of my gunshot wounds. I
kept walking, and I learned with every step that, as difficult as it is,
one *must* take the next step. Often you have to force yourself to do it.
In the jungle in South America on that November day, it was not my
turn to die, but certainly now was my time to live.

Life Gives No Guarantees

*Inspiration is disturbing. She does not believe in guarantees or insurance
or strict schedules. Yet, she will be there when you need her, but you have
to take it on trust. She knows when you need her better than you do.*
—J. Ruth Gendler, artist (1954—   )

I survived the massacre in Guyana and went on to marry an emergency room physician. I was also elected to serve in the California
legislature. We had our first child, and life was turning out to be just
as I had dreamed. We tried for more children, but after two miscarriages, a failed adoption, and fertility treatments, Steve and I decided
to give up on our dream of another child. I launched a statewide
campaign in California to be elected secretary of state. Miraculously,
three months later, I found myself pregnant in what doctors termed
a high-risk pregnancy. I promptly withdrew from the campaign to
focus on the health of our unborn child.

On a rainy January day, three months into my pregnancy, I was
en route to Sacramento. My secretary tracked me down, as police
had informed her that Steve had been in a car accident. I immediately
phoned the emergency room and talked with the attending physician.

I could tell by his voice that my husband's injuries were severe. I was an hour away, and as I rushed back to the Bay Area, I feared the worst.

Once I got to the hospital, it seemed like hours before they would let me see Steve. When I finally got to see him in the ICU, he had a shunt in his head and was on a respirator. His body was warm, but the machines indicated he had no brain function. I kissed him. I held him. I told him I loved him, even though I knew he couldn't hear me.

I couldn't believe the nightmare that was unfolding in front of me. I later learned that an uninsured driver with faulty brakes had careened through a stop sign, broadsiding Steve's car. His careless-ness had killed this talented, caring, vital man. I was now a pregnant widow with a young son.

The loss of my husband was traumatic. I no longer even wanted to get out of bed. Yet, I really had no choice. I was the sole supporter of two children, one yet unborn. Because we didn't have life insur-ance on Steve, I was financially destroyed. I had to sell everything, including my home. I spent the next eight years as a single mother raising two children.

Today, eleven years later, I am fortunate to live with great joy and happiness. I am married to a wonderful man, Barry Dennis. I met Barry on a blind date; he was a confirmed bachelor. Five months later, we were engaged!

I want women to remember that when life leaves them alone on the tarmac—whether it be the devastating loss of a loved one, the shattering of a lifelong dream, the loss of a job, or events that turn the world upside down—women can always learn to walk again. I am living proof that women can reinvent and rebuild their lives, no matter what hardships they have faced.

4. When life is not what you ordered, begin again.

I've learned that no matter what happens, or how bad it seems today that life does go on, and it will be better tomorrow. This I am certain.
— Dr. Maya Angelou, writer and poet (1928–)

I'll Beat Those Odds, Even on a Radiation Diet
Someone once described me as a swan. I look so smooth going across the lake, but underneath, I'm paddling like crazy.
— Shelly Lazarus, CEO, Ogilvy and Mather (1947–)

"You must be mistaken," I said, clearly and assertively informing the doctor of his error. "Stanley, I'd like a second opinion. I'd like the best radiologist to take another X-ray."

I am Jan Yanehiro, and those were my brave-sounding words. But that's all they were—just words—simply a front for the fear and jumbled thoughts inside me. I had just been told that my husband had a brain tumor.

I remember walking into the room to view the X-rays. I never expected to see the tumor so clearly. It was round, the size of a golf ball, surrounded by a blurry mass of tissue the size of a fist. "I see it . . . ," I said quietly. It was obvious no second opinion would be needed.

My husband, John Zimmerman, was forty-five years old and solidly built—220 pounds on a light day with the wind blowing, I always kidded. "Can you believe this?" John asked me. "A brain tumor?!"

The words—that condition—how foreign. It just didn't belong in our family. "No, I don't believe it," I said. And I vaguely remember thinking that John was going to be the miracle, the survivor of this ugly thing, and I was going to do a television story on it. Such wishful, silly thinking.

John was operated on the day after the X-ray diagnosis. The surgeon called me after the four-hour operation. "It's not a good tumor." I remember thinking, "Is any tumor good?" They got as much of the tumor as they could, but they could not get all of it. The mass was located behind his right eye. In simple terms, John was given a right frontal lobotomy. In removing the tumor, they had also removed the "silent" portion of his brain, the portion that governs emotion and behavior.

John's tumor had a name. It was called a *Glioblastoma multiforma,* stage 4. I could barely pronounce it at the time, let alone spell it. Today, I know all about it. Glioblastoma is a malignant tumor. There are four "grades" or "stages"—4 is tops, the most aggressive of the tumors. I kidded John that it was very appropriate that he have this type of tumor, being a "Type A" personality. You know the type: they work hard, they play hard, they live, challenge, and enjoy every aspect of life. John fought bravely. "Don't worry," he would say, "I'm going to beat this thing."

Our daughters sent get-well notes to their dad in the hospital. Jaclyn, twelve, wrote, "You have to get better, because I want you to meet your grandchildren one day!" Jenna, ten, wrote, "Daddy, I want you to get better, because you have to walk me down the aisle at my wedding." There followed seven weeks of daily radiation, second opinions, the recommendation of another operation, chemotherapy pills, anger, pain, and even humor. He lost seventy pounds on his radiation diet—a diet, he would joke, that he just couldn't recommend.

Just three days shy of six months, John lost the battle and his personal war. He was forty-six years old when he died at our home. Our children were twelve, ten, and six years young. It was raw. That's the word that keeps coming up again and again to describe John's dying.

Clinging to the Tiniest Speck of Hope

I wanted a perfect ending. Now I've learned, the hard way, that some
poems don't rhyme, and some stories don't have a clear beginning, middle,
and end. Life is about not knowing, having to change, taking the moment
and making the best of it without knowing what's going to happen next.
—Gilda Radner, comedian (1946–1989)

Just when I had thought all was great with the universe and everything was looking pretty darn good—*wham!*—death interfered.
Looking back, the signs were all there. We just didn't know it. John
had always had headaches. We just didn't pay attention when they
began to get worse. He crashed his car, an accident. He would get
up at 2 A.M. and take four Tylenol tablets because his headaches were
so bad. He had a cold that lasted for months and months. Stress, we
thought. He had always had a temper, but it had gotten shorter and
shorter. And he had always had a big laugh. We just never noticed that
we heard it less and less. Life was just so full, with three kids, careers,
travel, family, and friends.

When John was operated on, the surgeon said the tumor had
been growing for at least a year, possibly longer. Odd thing about living with someone you know is dying—you cling to the tiniest bit of
hope. If John was having a lucid moment, I thought, "Aha! He's beating
the odds." The doctor said at one point that the tumor hadn't grown
and the radiation seemed to be working. Break out the champagne!

In his last week, John lay dying on a rented hospital bed in the
family room of our home. He wore diapers, was given morphine
to dull the excruciating pain, and was fed applesauce by a nurse's
aide. He never got up from the bed. On the last night of his life, our
twelve-year-old daughter was at her seventh grade school dance. We
had to pick her up early, because we knew John's death was immi-
nent. Her friends all cried.

Relief is the word that describes how I felt when he died—relief to know John's agony was over, relief to know that my kids, our family, could once again find a "new" normal routine. And I never had a doubt in my mind that the lives of my children would go on. In fact, during John's last moments, I whispered to him that I would make sure that our children's lives would go on, and that I would do my best to make sure of this. This was my promise to him.

After six months of anger, fear, disbelief, chemotherapy, radiation, and uncertainty, I felt strangely calm. *Acceptance* is another word that comes to mind. At John's memorial service, we celebrated his life. I asked special friends to say only funny things about John. I insisted on a closed casket. The John who suffered from this brain tumor was not the John I chose to remember. He had become emaciated. To this day, I refuse to look at pictures of him when he battled cancer. On top of his casket, I placed all his favorite things: chocolate chip brownies by Mrs. Fields Cookies, poker chips because he loved the game, a picture of him deep sea fishing. His secretary sang the Tina Turner song "Simply the Best." John was gone.

You've heard that old cliché, "Time heals all." I don't think time heals. But months, years later, the grief and the sharp edges of John's death are softer.

In the months following John's death, I was faced with four lawsuits. John did not have enough life insurance. (He always felt he could do more with the money himself than if he paid for some life insurance policy.) He had half a million dollars in life insurance; he also had half a million dollars in an outstanding line of credit at a bank that had to be paid. I did not have a job. The television contract I had ended two months before John died. Now I was not only a widow but also an unemployed one.

In a strange way, the learning I had to do to resolve the lawsuits and my career was empowering. It took me years, lots of attorneys, and thousands of dollars to clean up the financial mess. More than one friend asked if I was angry with John for leaving me in such a state. No, I can't say I was ever angry, because John didn't want to die, and he never intended to leave me with lawsuits or a financial tangle.

Today, many years later, I am remarried and have five children in what some might call a ready-made family created with my husband, Robert Eves. Many people call my new family "The Brady Bunch." While that was a terrific television show, our real life is very different. We have weathered family counseling, family trips, family arguments, family disappointments, and new family traditions. We have seen our kids through high school, drug rehab, and college.

I live what I deem to be an adventurous, challenging life, one that proves that even in the darkest of circumstances, when life is not what you ordered, you can learn to begin again.

5. Learn the secrets of the blue-haired lady.

Honor wears different coats to different eyes.
　　—Barbara Tuchman, Pulitzer Prize—winning writer (1912–1989)

Her Hair Was Always Blue on Fridays
I was so far from the seat of power, but my naïveté worked to my advantage. When I was told that the studio passed on my first pilot, I thought that was a good thing—you know, like "passed" in college.
　　—Linda Bloodworth-Thomason, TV producer and writer (1947–　)

I wondered if he noticed her blue hair. He concealed all knowledge of the fact that the elderly woman sitting across from him in his opulent banker's office had just about the bluest hair he had ever seen.

I am Deborah Stephens, and the blue-haired lady was my grand-mother.

Her blue hair, combined with a matter-of-fact demeanor, penetrating eyes, and down-home Southern hospitality, left no doubt that he, Mr. Banker, was just a minor obstacle standing between her and what she wanted. She was there to obtain a loan. It never occurred to her that there were obstacles: her lack of collateral—her home wasn't in her name— no credit rating, and the fact that in those days (a mere thirty-two years ago), a woman could not even have a credit card in her own name. I knew Mr. Banker was no match for the blue-haired lady.

I had known her all my life, and I can swear that her silver mop of hair was always tinted blue on Fridays. It was her treat to herself—a tint, a curl, and a comb-out every Friday morning, no matter what. The whole process left her feeling beautiful, powerful, and bold. And so I came to love the blue hair almost as much as I loved her. I also grew up believing that all confident women of a certain age tinted their hair blue!

That day, in Mr. Banker's office, was a defining moment for me. Yes, my grandmother received the loan that day—a college student loan, for me. My grandmother's negotiation skills could blow the doors open in any corporate boardroom today. Yet she was uneducated and poor. Her wealth came in the form of deep religious beliefs and unconditional kindness. She also possessed the tenacity of a bulldog, as she never let the word "No" stand in her way.

What my grandmother lacked in cash she made up for in an over-abundance of dreams. She had an unrelenting belief in me, greater than any belief I held about myself. No matter the circumstances or challenges, she was determined that I would go places in life that she and my mother had only dreamed about.

Thanks to the blue-haired lady's meeting with Mr. Banker, I was college bound. The first female in two generations to apply, I had always seen college as an unattainable dream. Too big of a dream to imagine. Yet my grandmother *always* dealt in possibilities.

After college, I landed an exciting corporate job with a major publishing company, traveled the world, and made more money in a year than my mother had made in ten. Years later, I cofounded a management consulting firm and wrote six business books that were translated into eight different languages. Consulting with corporations and government, I worked with some of America's most powerful leaders. I was a faculty member in the prestigious executive development course at Stanford University and a guest lecturer. I lived in a part of the world that was closed to my grandmother and mother. Yet those two women were my inspiration and were most responsible for my success.

Every woman should have a blue-haired lady in her life. She is the woman who thinks you are terrific even when you don't feel terrific. The woman who always believes that anything is possible, no matter the odds. The one who continues to show you that life is a wondrous adventure even in the midst of great despair.

Defining Moments Are Possibilities Masquerading as Obstacles

One of the things I learned the hard way is that it doesn't pay to get discouraged.

—Lucille Ball, actress and comedian (1911–1989)

Obstacles and possibilities have often melded together to form defining moments in my life. My first defining moment occurred in the bank where I observed my grandmother negotiate a college loan for me. Defining moments also have a way of striking just when we think we have life figured out. Smartly compartmentalized lives can be turned upside down in a matter of moments.

Defining moment number two made its visit nearly seven years ago, and its subject was my husband of twenty-five years. A healthy, stocky, and robust man, Mike had always been full of life. One day, after playing a round of golf, he was unable to walk. The pain came in muscle spasms throughout his body. Thus, we began a multitude of journeys to the University of California-San Francisco Medical Center to unravel the illness that was ravaging his body.

The medical detective work took six months. In that time, my husband had lost 50 percent of his lung capacity. There were days when his fingers and toes ached so badly that he would dunk them into buckets of ice water to numb the pain. Hospitalized for a lung biopsy, he ended up on life support in the ICU unit of the local hospital. His diagnosis began with the term "pulmonary fibrosis, caused by derma-tomyositis and polymyositis"—words I could neither pronounce nor understand. We were told that the median survival rate was 5.5 years. The doctors recommended he consider a lung transplant.

I remember sitting in the fourteenth-floor waiting room while my husband was being examined by an entire team of doctors. Look-ing out the large window, I saw the Golden Gate Bridge. As I looked at the bridge, enrapt in its breathtaking beauty, I wondered if there was some way for me to escape all the medicine, the doctors, the tests, the daily battles with the insurance company, and this illness.

Tears rolled down my face. Why couldn't I just have a normal life? How do you even prepare yourself or your family for the prospect of a lung transplant? The ring of my cell phone interrupted my thoughts. It was my daughter's kindergarten teacher. Could I please come pick her up, as she and fifteen of her classmates had head lice? Head lice! I'm talking to surgeons about lung transplants, and we haven't even figured out how to rid the world of head lice! "What would the blue-haired lady do? How would she manage all of this?" I wondered.

Today, Mike has lived longer than anyone expected him to. As he battles the odds, his spirit reminds me of my grandmother's. When you live with someone who wages war against a life-threatening illness, even the most ordinary of days become special. Illness teaches many lessons—lessons in love, faith, courage, optimism, and hope. The experience has also taught me much about the role of patience and the mysteries inherent in life.

DEBORAH CHECKED AGAIN, BUT THERE WERE NO EASY ANSWERS.

Before Mike's illness, I was quite an impatient person, always pushing and striving to make things happen as quickly and succinctly as possible. Surrounded by to-do lists and calendars and planners, I believed that I could control and manage everything that life threw my way. I've learned now that control is an illusion and that patience is the virtue your mother always told you it was. The things we think we have control over in life often have a sneaky way of showing us our lack of control. For, in just one moment, entire lives can change forever. Yet I am proof that those changes—the defining moments— hold the opportunities to live a life filled with purpose. They are the lessons the blue-haired lady taught me.

6. When you are standing at the edge of the pool, jump in.

I read and walked for miles at night along the beach, writing bad verse and searching endlessly for someone wonderful who would step out of the darkness and change my life. It never crossed my mind that person could be me.
　　—Anna Quindlen, writer (1953–   )

Hide and Seek
The willingness to accept responsibility for one's own life is the source from which self-respect springs.
　　—Joan Didion, writer (1934–   )

As a child, and into adulthood, I learned to hide my light from others so that no one would notice and hurt me. Perhaps it came from being sexually abused, and learning that people can take very special parts of you without your permission. As a result of this abuse, I developed a fear that someone would take that very special part of me and destroy it. I decided to hide it.

　　I am Michealene Cristini Risley, and I became an expert at hide and seek. The childhood game followed me into adulthood. I became so good at hiding myself; it took so much of my energy that it stopped me from focusing on what I wanted in life. I hid my talents because I did not want people to notice and hurt me or take away those gifts. Little did I know that this was impossible. I would work my way through life, getting close to all of the things that I dreamed of but avoided or had fallen short of. I had wanted to write and direct movies since I was a kid. I can remember the day, I was probably twelve, when I told my mother that I was going to be a writer, and promptly went out to the corner store and purchased a notepad.

In my career, I took jobs that circled around those desires, but never let me touch them—to get directly into that role. I stared longingly from the edge, hoping for what seemed so out of my reach. The experience was like having your swimsuit on at the edge of the pool but never having the courage to jump in. I secretly hoped that someone would grab my hand and help me into the water. What I needed most was for someone to tell me that it was okay to want those things, it was okay to dream and be—and that I wasn't a child anymore. That as an adult, no one could take those gifts away from me. My fantasy was always that this person would grab me by the hand and nurture those talents, while protecting me. My own inner voices were hard to conquer. How dare I hope for things in my life? How dare I dream so large? And yet, my own voices did not stop success. I was very successful. Friends and family would look at my career and marvel at how happy and successful I was. I was the only one that knew the truth. I was still standing at the edge waiting to jump in.

A Family Full of Secrets

Find out what you don't want to know about yourself, what you're afraid of, and then face it head on.
    —Linda Evans, actress (1942–   )

In 1968 the Detroit Tigers won the World Series, and my dad lost his father. Death was always part of my childhood. When Grandfather

Dominic passed away, I was eight. I remember the funeral service. The priest kept ringing the mass bell, and my cousin, thinking it was the ice cream man, kept asking for a strawberry push-up. We tried not to snicker as her voice got louder and more demanding. Somehow along the way, I came to believe that if you told your parents bad things, it would cause their deaths. It was a difficult belief to have inside a family already full of secrets. Imagine having such a secret, that you thought would kill your parents—it immobilizes you. Forget the pool, you don't even walk outside.

It was when I was facing life and death at the same time that I finally did walk outside. I gave birth to my first child the same day that my father had a brain tumor removed. Life and death. They seem always to be intertwined. I couldn't travel to see my dad, and I didn't know if he would make it out of surgery alive. I had to try to find a way to celebrate the gift I was receiving: a healthy baby boy. It was bittersweet.

Three weeks after the birth of my first son, I had the chance to see my father alive, and he got to see his eleventh grandson. I studied my father's face. It lit up with joy at his first glimpse of my son. It dawned on me that my dad's life would end soon. We spent an evening playing skit-skat together while he was in the ICU. His room smelled of antiseptic. It was a quiet night after a day of indignities that my father had handled with patience and dignity. We played for keeps that night. When I won, I took a cigarette from his pack, hoping that it would slow the speed with which he would die. If he won, he got a cigarette to add to his pile. Even with aphasia, he could count faster than I could. He knew when I cheated. We shared laughter.

Later that evening, I stood at the foot of the bed as he turned to me and called out the name "Mary Jane." This was my childhood friend's name. I froze. Yes, I had always wanted to confront my father, but could this possibly be the moment? I spent years rehearsing this

conversation. Not now, not when he was dying. Yet, here he was trying to talk about it. I agonized over what I should do. I wanted to run
for the nearest exit.

All The Rage of Mount St. Helens

*You can stand tall without standing on someone. You can be a victor
without having victims.*
— *Harriet Beecher Stowe, activist and writer (1811–1896)*

Standing in the intensive care unit, I felt transported back in time.
There was the puke-green tile that framed the large mirror on the
kitchen wall. I could hear the crackle of the olive oil heating up in the
frying pan. I felt terror engulf me as I approached my mother. With her
hands deep in the sudsy water and her back to me, she whirled around
as I said, "Mom, Mary Jane says Dad put his hand down her pants."

My mother exploded with all the rage of Mount St. Helens
and glared down at me. "How could you ever think that your father
would do something like that?"

I stopped. How could I think that? What was wrong with me? If
Mom did not believe that Dad had done that to Mary Jane, how would
she ever believe what he had done to me? I felt great big waves of nothing crashing over me like tons of needles prickling through my body,
making me numb. I was still standing, but my mind had gone away.

The memories of those moments in the kitchen seared my mind
as I stood at the foot of my dad's deathbed. I looked closely at my
father. Did I have the courage? Did he have the strength? Was this fair
for me to do now, or ever? Here was my chance, and I had become
that young girl again, waiting for someone to take my hand, unable
to string a coherent word together. Afraid. The opportunity passed.

In the last few days of my dad's life, his six children alternated
visits, keeping him company. At my turn, I sat in a chair next to him

reading from the bible. It was a passage that I knew well. Not because I read the Bible frequently, but because my father had a humorous poster of these words hung in his office for years. "Yea, though I walk through the valley of death, I shall fear no evil." I added the words that he had on the bottom of his poster: "For I am the meanest son of a bitch in the valley!" Can someone chuckle without any movement? I think so.

Each of us took time to say good-bye. Even though he was in a coma, the nurses told us he would be able to hear until the end. When it was my turn, I curled up on the bed next to him and whispered in his ear, "Dad, we both made mistakes, and I am sorry for that. I forgive you." I felt the tension leave his body.

I wasn't in the room when my father died, but his spirit was still there when I arrived. I could feel it. I reached into my back pocket for the lottery tickets I had purchased. My older sister took one and I took the other. I felt the familiar recognition of his flat fingernail as I took his hand. We both stood holding his thumbs and had him scratch the tickets. His body was still warm. I could hear my father's silent laugh echo through the room—both tickets were winners.

It was within these last few days; with stark clarity I realized that I was no longer that abused child. I had made a choice some time ago to hide myself, and by continuing to hide into adulthood, I became the abuser . . . of myself. Through my father's struggle with death and becoming a mother, I realized that those actions were no longer how I defined myself. I remember thinking that these were events that happened and they no longer define who I am or how much I deserve in life. Enough. It was in that moment of clarity I was able to break free of the past and to fully jump into my life without fear.

Today, I am happily married and have three young boys. I am proof that women can endure, can turn obstacles and heartbreak into opportunities that can lead to a wondrous life. In 2003, I resurrected a lifelong dream to write and direct my first short film called *Flashcards*. It is a film about child sexual abuse, much of it is my own story, the story of a young girl who is sexually molested and afraid to talk about it. My depiction of sexual abuse, a huge epidemic in our country, concerns the fear of repercussions mingled with the love and the shame and confusion. It is a story that is repeated throughout seemingly "normal" homes. Child sexual abuse is the least reported form of abuse. The statistic is understandable, given the confusion about the perpetrators, many of whom are relatives or friends. My message to women who may have similar life experiences as mine: Go ahead, hold your nose, close your eyes, and simply jump forward into your life!

The WIT Kit
Exercises and Tools for Managing Misfortunate Events

You can clutch your past so tightly to your chest that
it leaves your arms too full to embrace the present.
— Jan Glidewell, journalist

1. Find yourself a beautiful journal and label it "My WIT Kit." Now grab a favorite pen and open to the first page. Write down three things you want to experience or accomplish in your lifetime. You may be thinking, "Right now, I just want to get through the day." We understand. But this is your place to dream, your opportunity to think big. Consider this a gift to yourself. In your WIT Kit journal you have the freedom to look ahead instead of being bogged down in the present. Please don't censor yourself. You can be as frivolous or as idealistic as you'd like.

---

2. Think of just one thing you can do this week to make progress on one of those three dreams. If you want to go back to college and get your degree, maybe you can pick up the phone and ask your local college to mail you registration requirements and a course catalog. If you want to want to travel to Europe, you can go online and check out available deals on travel Web sites. If you want to ride horses, you can visit a local stable and ask about their lessons or trail rides. If you want to open your own store, you can order the free booklets that are available from the Small Business Administration. Write your idea down.

No matter how overwhelmed you are right now, doing one thing to make progress on those three dreams will help move you out of any depressing mood. Every Sunday, review your three dreams and the action steps you have taken. Report in to your kitchen table group. If you got overloaded this week and didn't follow up on your intentions, just ask yourself what one specific action you're going to take this week.

3. Get into the habit of writing in your WIT Kit journal every day, even if you only scribble a few lines. It's easiest to make it a habit if you choose a time of day to write. Maybe while you're sipping your morning tea, or for ten minutes before bed.

Believe us—this investment will pay off for you in many ways. Writing in your journal is a gift you give yourself—a way to release doubts and fears onto the page, to avoid losing sight of your hopes and dreams. Your WIT Kit journal is a place to express yourself so that you don't bottle up emotions. You will be able to note progress and have a visible record of where you are now and where you were a short while ago.

chapter two

Learning to Love the "Oops"

7. Be willing to make great mistakes.

Mistakes are a part of the dues one pays for a full life. . . .
— *Sophia Loren, Italian actress (1934–   )*

The Theory of the "Oops"
Something good always comes out of a failure or a great mistake.
— *Albert Einstein, German-born physicist (1879–1955)*

Last year Jan and Deborah attended a conference hosted by one of Silicon Valley's venture capitalists. One session they attended was called "Wisdom Learned." The panelists, four chief executive officers (all men), spent fifty minutes sharing the insights they had learned from mistakes they had made during their careers. Several days later, a prominent business newspaper ran a story about a high-technology CEO who had "heroically" admitted his mistakes and moved forward. The reporter referred to the CEO's authenticity and brilliance at admitting his errors! The irony was not lost on Jan and Deborah. What successful men call wisdom, women too often label as mistakes.

Smart people learn as much, if not more, from mistakes as they do from successes. Thomas Edison failed thirty-seven times before inventing the lightbulb. Babe Ruth struck out at bat 348 times. Mistakes in scientific laboratories have resulted in 3M's Post-it Notes, CorningWare, and Botox! In our own lives, success has often been the artful management of our mistakes.

Months later, we were asked to speak at a large women's conference on a topic of our choice. Jan suggested that we speak about our "best mistakes." We thought she needed a sanity check, but we trusted Jan's intuition, so we were prepared to follow her down this path. After all, everyone's lives are filled with mistakes. Perhaps we ought to start talking about them, bringing them out of their hidden spaces and shining light onto the "oops."

The day of the conference, more than 600 women showed up to participate. The workshop was so successful that we were asked to repeat it at the California Governor's Conference on Women that same year.

The Female "Oops" Center

Making a damn fool of yourself is absolutely essential. So, whatever you want to do, just do it. Don't be stifled by the fear of a good mistake.
   —*Gloria Steinem, activist and writer (1934–   )*

Researchers at Vanderbilt University have identified a part of the human brain that recognizes when a person has made a mistake. Scientists say this brain region becomes very active when we begin to make a mistake. In fact, this "oops center" isn't just detecting that we're about to make an error; it's trying to prevent it!

We're convinced that women are best equipped to capitalize on our oops centers, because we are more open and willing to share our mistakes with others. Why is sharing important, you might ask? Aren't we supposed to downplay our mistakes and exude that confident, poised, "got it all together" routine? Well, yes and no.

If Scientists Can Get Excited about Mistakes, Smart Women Can Too

If I thought it was the right thing to do, I was for it regardless of the outcome.
   —*Golda Meir, former Prime Minister of Israel (1898–1978)*

After a decade of shelving studies that either failed or ended in negative results, Dr. Bjorn Olsen at Harvard University saw the value in a few good mistakes—a worldwide collection of mistakes, to be exact. In 2002, Olsen created the *Journal of Negative Results,* which focuses only on scientific studies that do not work. One might think that Dr. Olsen's approach to science is a little askew or even depressing. After all, what scientist would want to publish his or her biggest mistakes and failures in a national journal? Surprisingly, thousands did, including many leading researchers tackling HIV, the cure for cancer, and other important work. Why? Scientists view negative outcomes and mistakes as stepping-stones to answers.

They willingly share information about their mistakes so other scientists can avoid making the same ones. Science is based on trial and error.

Over time, the four of us have learned to adopt this "scientific approach" to mistakes. Instead of dreading them, hiding them, or being embarrassed by them, we understand that mistakes are doorways to discovery. We have come to understand that by willingly sharing our mistakes, we help both ourselves and other women.

In the next stories, we share what we've learned from some of the common mistakes that women make. We hope that by reading these, you can avoid making those same mistakes. If you've already made them, at least you'll know you are not alone.

8. Give up thinking that you can do it all.

To live is so startling it leaves little time for anything else.
— Emily Dickinson, poet (1830–1886)

You've Come a Long Way, Baby
I'm having trouble managing the mansion. What I need is a wife.
— Ella Tambussi Grasso, first woman governor in the United States
(1919–1981)

Sometime during the past four decades, from bra burnings in the '70s to marches on the White House lawn for the Equal Rights Amendment, many women began to take pride in the marketing slogan "You've come a long way, baby," and the delusional belief that they could do it all.

What made women think we could be Superwomen? Made us believe we could climb to the top and shatter the glass ceiling while bouncing children on our hips, maintaining perfectly immaculate homes, and doing our best to become intelligent and glamorous wives, girlfriends, and partners? Volunteering in churches and communities while making strides into leadership roles in the House, Senate, and corporate world, some very tired women have left the groundbreaking path of progress littered with well-worn shoes!

We believe that many women have been brainwashed into thinking we can have it all, do it all, and remain sane and serene in the process. We are here to tell you one simple truth: you cannot. We should know——we have all tried it and failed miserably in the process.

Among the four of us, we've traded in "have it all" for "have it all at different times." For us, it is simply a much better way to live.

"STRESS? WHAT STRESS?"

"Have it all at different times" thinking requires living your life based upon your own set of personal values. Whether you are single, married, a stay-at-home mom, or a mother who works outside the home doesn't matter. What matters is that you are a person who meets or exceeds your own values, not the values of others.

According to "have it all at different times" thinking, it does not matter if you are a corporate executive, corporate employee, or corporate wife. What matters is that you have designed your life around what fits best for you and those you care about.

Today's generation of women has more opportunities and choices than our great-grandmothers could ever have imagined. Ironically, many young women are choosing not to even try to "have it all." Jackie sponsors a teen conference for young women each year. Many of these young women have told us they grew up watching their mothers work long hours and lead very unbalanced lives. These young women are adamant about their choice to not struggle like their mothers did. They are very clear that they will focus on a few top priorities instead of rushing from one thing to the next. Wise words, we think, gleaned from the mouths of very young women.

Find Fifteen Minutes

How we spend our days is, of course, how we spend our lives.
  —Annie Dillard, writer (1945–   )

Do you take care of everyone but yourself? Is your life stressful? If you're like many women, your honest answer to the second question will be "Yes." Do you carry around a subconscious belief that putting yourself first is a selfish way to live? If you answered "Yes," it's time to take baby steps toward honoring your own rights and needs instead of everyone else's. You don't want to look back with regret at your life and wish that you had slowed down and appreciated what really mattered.

Starting today, carve out a minimum of fifteen minutes a day of time to call your own. Do this even if you have to wake early in the morning or stay up late at night to find the time. During that time, take a walk, listen to beautiful music, read a novel, or do anything that connects you to the quietness of life. You will be surprised how rejuvenated you can feel even after only fifteen minutes of solitude.

9. Create "to-don't" lists.

Death and taxes and childbirth: there is never any convenient time for any of them.
　　　—Margaret Mitchell, author of Gone with the Wind *(1900–1949)*

Misguided Pride in Multitasking
For fast-acting relief, try slowing down.
　　　—Lily Tomlin, comedian and actress *(1939–　)*

"When my children were both toddlers," said Deborah, "my routine mirrored that of countless moms: waking at the crack of dawn, filling bottles with formula, packing diaper bags, and heading off to a day care center. I would drop off my children and drive to work, all before 7:30 A.M. The night before was always filled with laundry, dirty dishes that needed washing, and children's playtime. Weekends were designated for cleaning house, grocery shopping, and errands. Exhaustion was my normal mode of operating.

"One day, I caught a cold. If I missed work, I thought, there would be too much to catch up on, so I continued my routine, but added another element. Instead of having lunch during the day, I went home and took a thirty-minute nap because I felt so badly. After three weeks of this routine, I ended up in the emergency room and was diagnosed with pneumonia. My mistake of taking care of everyone but myself led to many days of missed work, chores that piled up at home, and disruption in the lives of everyone around me. I learned that I needed to start taking care of myself with the same passion I took in caring for others."

Are You on the List?

It is not where you begin; it is where you end that counts.
   ——Faith Littlefield, writer

"It all began," Michealene said, "with the dreaded pink note my three young boys brought home from school. It's the note that makes any mother shudder—head lice has struck the classroom! Each night I checked the boys' heads and soon discovered that indeed we had the dreaded visitors.

"Now I was stripping sheets off of four beds daily, vacuuming, dusting, and disinfecting nearly 'round the clock while I checked the heads of the boys, my husband, and even the dogs! This routine went on for nearly two weeks. Finally, our living quarters and all its occupants seemed to be cleared of the tiny enemies. We headed off to Lake Tahoe for a weekend vacation. I was absolutely exhausted and looked forward to a weekend in the woods.

"During our second day in the woods, I began to feel ill. I also found tender lumps behind my ears and in my armpits. I grew very concerned. As the day progressed, I started running a mild fever. We left the campsite for the local hospital.

"I sat in the emergency room thinking of twenty-five terrible diseases I just knew I had. I thought of my children and my husband. How would they manage without me? I had already jumped to the conclusion that the symptoms and swollen glands in my armpits and behind my ears could only be the big C-word—cancer.

"The doctor on duty thoroughly assessed me. He drew some blood and told me he would have the results in an hour. As we waited, I grew even more concerned and had convinced myself that certainly I was dying.

"'Mrs. Risley,' the nurse said, breaking my concentration on the thoughts of my impending doom. 'The doctor would like to see you now.' I entered the room and looked at the doctor with what could only be an expression of sheer terror. The doctor looked back at me and said, 'My suspicions are confirmed, Mrs. Risley. You have one of the worse cases of head lice I've seen in twenty-five years. The swelling in your lymph glands are due to an allergic reaction you are having to the louse bites.'

"Head lice! No cancer, no life-threatening disease?

"I had forgotten to put myself on my 'to-do' list. I had ignored my own symptoms because I was too busy worrying about everyone else. I had checked everyone in the household—even the dogs—but I had never once checked myself. My mistake was creating a to-do list that didn't include me!"

Discard the Lists!

I hate housework! You make the beds, you do the dishes—and six months later you have to start all over again.
    —Joan Rivers, comedian (1933–)

We take care of the kids, the dog, the cat, the partner, the coworkers, the team, the in-laws. Look at any woman's to-do list and the word *me* will be conspicuously absent. We don't get enough sleep even though we need a good eight hours. We eat on the run and cram every minute of every hour with something to do, say, make, or be. Many of us seem to take pride in multitasking. We admire people who cram as much as they can in each day.

Please, enough of this. It's killing us—literally. We have to move ourselves nearer to the top of the list or we won't be in the state of mind or physical shape to take care of ourselves and those who need us the most.

Author and management consultant Tom Peters suggests it's time to turn our to-do list into a "to-don't" list. We agree.

HOW *DOES* SHE DO IT?

We need to rid our to-do lists of things that don't matter, don't create value, don't make a difference. We need to restructure our lives and take more time to do things that bring us joy. Women need to carve out time for the activities that will create meaningful lives and discard the things that won't.

Think about this tomorrow morning when you compile your to-do list. What two things can you take off that really don't have to be done? Maybe you can order takeout after your long day of work instead of fixing a fancy meal. Maybe it's more important to take your children to the park than to mop the floor. Perhaps you can ask someone else to organize the office party instead of doing it all by yourself.

What can you do to turn your to-do list into a "don't-have-to-do" list?

10. Never underestimate yourself.

Never bend your head. Always hold it high and look the world straight in the eye.
    ——*Helen Keller, writer (1880–1968)*

I Was Always Polite and Waited for My Turn
There is only one real sin, and that is to persuade oneself that the second-best is anything but second-best.
    ——*Doris Lessing, British writer (1919–   )*

Early in her career, Jackie spent many hours of wasted time in self-doubt. She consistently underestimated herself. "I struggled at the time to hide my self-doubt and to appear strong. A year after I lost the seat for Congress (in 1979), I ran against a twenty-year incumbent for a post on the County Board of Supervisors, and I beat him by 18,000 votes. The experiences showed me that I could rally people and that they would believe in me and support me.

"Years later in the State Assembly, I continued to make the same mistake of underestimating myself and allowing self-doubt to cloud my vision. I had very strong opinions about gun control. I knew first-hand the tragedy these guns caused people," said Jackie. "However, I was reluctant to carry any legislation on banning assault weapons, because I was told by advisors and colleagues that to do so would mean the end of my political career. 'Jackie,' they said, 'the National Rifle Association will come after you. They'll spend millions of dollars to defeat you.'

"In a tiny moment of strength, in the midst of all who told me 'No,' I decided to coauthor legislation to ban assault weapons in the state of California. Standing at the podium in the legislative cham-

MISGUIDED MUGS

DON'T WORRY, THEY'LL TAKE CARE OF YOU.

IGNORE YOUR INNER VOICE.

TAKE CARE OF EVERYONE BUT YOURSELF.

FEAR MISTAKES.

UNDERESTIMATE YOURSELF.

FEAR CONFRONTATION, AVOID CONFLICT.

NETWORK AND SEEK FRIENDS ONLY WHEN DESPERATE.

THINK YOU CAN DO IT ALL.

TO SUCCEED BE MORE "LIKE A MAN."

COMMON MISTAKES WOMEN MAKE
(AVOID COLLECTING THE WHOLE SET)

bers, I was in the midst of debating the toughest anti-gun legislation in the United States. A colleague took the podium, interrupted me, and asked condescendingly, 'Ms. Speier, have you ever shot an assault weapon?' Obviously he didn't know of my past. Stunned, I countered, 'No sir, but have you ever been shot at point-blank range by an assault weapon?' There was dead silence in the chamber. 'Well, I have, and that's why we need this legislation.' The bill overwhelmingly passed, and many television stations throughout the state reported on the heated exchange. That experience taught me to quit second-guessing myself."

Be Your Own Worst Enemy

It's not who you are that holds you back; it's who you think you're not.
      — Barbara Walters, journalist (1931–)

"I've had a tendency in the past," said Jackie, "to not question author-ity. Always being too polite, waiting my turn, and giving too much credence to those in power. I watched other people—less capable, less talented—succeed, while I sat in the stands and looked on. We do such a disservice to ourselves and those around us when we are our own worst enemy in this way."

A wise woman told us, "There is a terrible penalty to be paid for not using one's talent." Are you using your talents? Have you let other people talk you out of pursuing something you're good at? Have you bowed to pressure and abandoned a project that was meaningful to you?

Our ability to contribute to this world is directly proportional to our conviction that we have something of value to offer.

Vow not to be deterred by doubt—whether it's coming from you or someone around you. No one wins when we underestimate our capabilities. Identify something you strongly believe in, as Jackie did, and resolve that you will work toward making that a reality. Promise that you will move forward with conviction and courage instead of second-guessing yourself.

11. Don't wait until you are depressed or desperate (or both) to network.

The more I traveled, the more I realized that fear makes strangers of people who should be friends.
      — Shirley MacLaine, actress (1934–)

Make Time for Nurturing and Conversing

You should always know when you are shifting gears in life. You should leave your eras; they should never leave you.

———*Leontyne Price, Grammy-winning opera singer (1927–   )*

Anne Robinson built Windham Hill Records into a Grammy-winning multinational record company. In 1996 she sold the company to BMG and thought that she would continue in the role of chief executive officer. Instead, BMG exercised their option to buy her out.

"The company was my whole life for twenty-three years, and in one day it was over," said Anne. "I hid out and was depressed. Running a large company for twenty-three years left me little time for anyone, not even myself. I realized I was alone. I hadn't made the time to stay connected to my friends when I worked at Windham Hill. I suddenly realized how important those people were to me. I needed to be with people who cared about me."

If your job becomes your entire life and your job ends, you may not know what to do with yourself. If you haven't nurtured your friendships because you got caught up in your many work responsibilities, you could very well end up facing the change alone.

It can be easy to let our women friends go when we're busy. When we don't have a lot of time, for whatever reason, our women friends are the first ones we stop seeing. Perhaps we think we can count on them to "always be there." Perhaps we forget that friendships need to be kept current, that letting them languish is a sign of disrespect. Perhaps we don't know that maintaining a close bond with our women friends not only makes us feel better, but it just might save our lives.

"CHERYL, YOU'VE BEEN SEEING
YOUR FAMILY AGAIN, HAVEN'T YOU?"

Tend and Befriend

*Study after study has found that our social ties reduce our risk of disease.
There's no doubt that women friendships help us live longer.*
— Dr. Laura Cousin Klein, Penn State University

According to a landmark study recently conducted at UCLA, our
connections to women friends actually counteract the stress most of
us experience on a daily basis. Engaging in a "tending and befriending"
behavior counters stress in women and produces a calming effect.
Not only do our women friends soothe us, give us encouragement,
and help us remember who we really are, our friendships might well
even save our lives.

A famed Nurses' Health Study from Harvard Medical School found that the more women friends one had, the less likely the woman was to develop physical impairments as they aged and the more likely they were to lead a joyful and meaningful life. In fact, the results were so significant the researchers concluded that not having close friends or confidants was as detrimental to a woman's health as smoking or carrying extra weight. Don't let one more minute pass without reaching out to a woman friend. Build into your daily routine a way to connect with another woman.

12. Don't believe that to succeed you must be "more like a man."

For women there are undoubtedly great difficulties in the path but so much more to overcome. Being a woman is not one of them. First, no woman should say, "I am but a woman." What more can you dare ask for or dare to be?

> ——*Maria Mitchell, astronomer and first woman member of the American Academy of Arts and Sciences Hall of Fame (1818–1889)*

Think Like a Woman
Let the world know you as you are, not as you think you should be, because sooner or later, if you are posing, you will forget the pose, and then where are you?

> ——*Fanny Brice, comedian (1891–1951)*

In the late 1970s, Deborah traded a college campus for corporate life, where women learned quickly that success somehow came packaged in male clothing and mind-sets.

"It should never have happened to me. Very strong and highly intelligent women mentored me along. I had worked for the dean for women at my university, when she was one of the top twenty-five most powerful women in the country. I had also been a student of two pioneering researchers, Eleanor Maccoby and Carol Jacklin, who had just published their landmark book, *The Psychology of Sex Differences*. At twenty-three, I thought I was prepared, ready to take my place in corporate America with the confidence, knowledge, and support that would allow me to blaze a trail.

"In a matter of months I had lost my ability to think like a woman. Quickly, I learned what would be rewarded and what would not. One of only a few women in the culture, I didn't fit in, so I embarked upon a course that would 'fix me' in ways that I thought were needed. I kept a copy of the best-selling book *Games Mother Never Taught You* in my desk, rereading chapters and thinking that if I only tried, I could become more like *them*. I took classes and training to overcome what I thought were my inabilities.

"I began to dress differently, eschewing bright colors for button-down Oxford shirts and well-tailored suits. I cut my long hair short, and I even took a golf lesson, because all of the men I worked with played golf! I quit wearing makeup except for mascara—somehow I just couldn't part with the mascara! I learned to play poker and I read the sports page along with the *Wall Street Journal* just so I could take part in the office conversations.

"One day I reached my breaking point. Returning from a trip that had taken me to fifteen different cities in seven days, I found a note from my boss asking me to justify my airfare expense along with a question that was meant to be a joke: 'While in New York, did you get your shopping fix?'

"PARTNER WANNABE,
PASSED OVER AGAIN, LACKING
GOLF GAME AND THE BALLS."

HAIKU LOWDOWN

"That did it. I marched into my manager's office and told him that the entire company was made up of closed-minded men. I left his office, locked myself in a bathroom stall, and cried. Wiping the tears from my eyes and fixing the running mascara, I returned to my office, determined that no one would know my agony.

"The next day I was summoned to go to lunch with the president of our west coast division. I was certain I was going to be fired. Placing me squarely in the catbird seat, he grilled me on why I thought the culture was sexist. 'Why do you think it is so difficult for you to succeed? Why do you feel uncomfortable?'

"'Why continue the charade?' I thought. I was going to be fired anyway, so I told him the truth. Much to my shock, he concluded the lunch by saying that he agreed with me. He told me he wanted my help and advice on changing the culture, which he saw as detrimental to long-term success. He said he wanted talent, and he didn't care what gender, race, or type it came in as long as it was human!

"Today, I wear makeup and do not own one Oxford button-down shirt. Heck, I even wear perfume! I make no apologies and I bring all of my talents to the table, not hiding them just because they are feminine. I am quick to recognize that when I don't fit in, it may not be me, but the culture.

"Now steeped in organizational systems, which I've studied for twenty years, I clearly see what was impossible for me to understand so many years ago. Cultures have a strong and homogenizing effect upon the people in the organization. Male-dominated cultures, over time, can make even the most competent and strong women begin to doubt themselves.

"Sadly though, the myth that we need to be more like men than women to succeed lives on. Liz Ryan, founder of World-Wit, an online community of over 40,000 professional women says 'its truly amazing that we can even dress ourselves! Look on any shelf in the bookstore or the myriad of training programs directed to women and one can see a lineup of products devoted to helping women fix what is wrong with them.'

"The skills and insights that women bring don't need to be changed or rearranged simply because they are feminine. They need to be embraced and celebrated by corporations and cultures. Instead of trying to fix our feminine selves to fit the male standard, perhaps we need to continue to change the world of work to allow, accept, and even seek the different ways we women communicate and lead. Surprisingly, in the organizations that are enlightened enough to recognize the value of this, something miraculous happens. Men grow too!"

13. Move on, move up, or move out.

You can do one of two things: just shut up. which is something I don't find easy, or learn an awful lot very fast and stand up for yourself!
—Jane Fonda, actress (1937–)

Don't Take It Personally, But . . .
Some people are molded by their admirations, others by their hostilities.
—Elizabeth Bowen, Irish writer (1899–1973)

Peggy Klaus produced and directed the *Tonight Show* for years. She said there were two things she heard from women that she never heard from men: "I've been humiliated," and "I've been betrayed."

Peggy says she has seen men scream at each other, stare each other down, and almost come to blows in a meeting. "Yet when the meeting ends, they slap each other on the back and go play golf. It would take two decades for women to forgive each other after something like that," says Peggy. "If I could find a pill that would not let us take things so personally, I would do it immediately and retire to an island."

Aversion to conflict and a tendency to take most things personally are all too common mistakes made by women. Confronting the people and the things in our life that we need to resolve in order to move on, move up, or move out can be uncomfortable. Yet avoiding those issues only makes us weak. By facing those issues head-on, we become stronger and more in control of our lives.

Many of us fear confrontation because of the unfair labels women seem to end up with: "she's a bitch," "she's a real ball-buster," "she's the ice queen," "she's the iron lady." Maybe men are able to use confrontation more effectively because they don't get stuck with these labels?

We're not advocating that we become like men, who shout and swear. Nor do we believe confrontation has to happen in loud, uncaring, and hostile ways. Yet we do advocate that every woman develop a set of tools for confronting people. We also need to be comfortable being on the receiving end of confrontation. Conflict resolution tools need to be a part of our organizational DNA.

We need to fully understand that disagreements are part of life and are to be expected when we're in any kind of relationship, from a marriage to a corporate merger. If we run from a disagreement, pretend it doesn't exist, or hide from it, we only hurt ourselves.

Have you ever seen a woman successfully stand up for herself and skillfully handle a disagreement? What did she do? Why did you admire the way she resolved that argument? How can you emulate her? Could you approach her and ask for her best-practice tips on dealing with difficult people?

Have you ever attended a seminar on negotiation? If you are like most of us, you haven't. Check with your professional association or the local adult education center to see if they have a workshop on negotiation and conflict resolution. A half-day program could be just what you need to start acquiring these all-important skills.

Is there an issue right now you need to confront or negotiate? Can you role-play that situation with your "kitchen table group" so you can practice your responses and develop your ability to think on your feet when dealing with aggression?

14. Trust in God, but row away from rocks.

An expert is a person who has made all of the mistakes that can be made in a very narrow field.
—Niels Bohr, Danish physicist (1885–1962)

I Trusted They Would Take Care of Me

Life doesn't accommodate you, but often shatters. Every seed destroys its container or else there would be no fruition anywhere on the earth.
— *Florida Scott Maxwell, writer (1883–1979)*

Jan Yanehiro trusted that the television station she had worked for (and made millions of dollars for) would take care of her after the show she had created was cancelled. After all, she had racked up an impressive set of ratings and three Emmys over a fifteen-year run with *Evening Magazine*. It was a beloved daily television program that came into the homes and hearts of millions of Californians.

In a matter of days, her contract with the network had dropped from $200,000 per year to $26,000. Jan learned quickly that all who promised they would "take care of her" disappeared when the cold, hard facts of the new contract were spelled out. "I was devastated," said Jan. "I trusted that this company, where I had spent most of my adult life, would somehow take care of me. It was a big mistake."

Nancy Pedot, former chief executive officer of a major retail conglomerate, was instrumental in taking the company from start-up to initial public offering in four short years. Appearing on the cover of *Business Week* and a darling of Wall Street, Nancy was a rare breed, a female chief executive officer of a publicly traded company—at the time, one of only three in the nation.

Nancy decided that her next goal was to spend more time with her teenage son. He would soon be on his way to college, and Nancy did not want to miss his remaining years at home. She resigned her position to the board of directors, trusting that those in charge would tell the truth about why she was leaving.

Without her permission or knowledge, the news of Nancy's departure was released in a manner that suggested she had been fired. Although Nancy was not sure of the rationale behind the decision, it did protect the stock from dropping, because, of course, Wall Street would never believe that a woman would leave a CEO position in order to spend more time with her family.

Nancy awoke to a barrage of television commentary and newspaper articles with stories of her dismissal. Imagine her surprise! Friends, former colleagues, and executives phoned Nancy and spoke as though tragedy had struck. When she attempted to tell the truth—that she had chosen to step down and had not been fired—only her closest friends believed her. Nancy had trusted that things would be handled in a respectful and ethical way. The media had told a different story.

Say Good Night to Cinderella

Now the Cinderella yearning tends to hit women after college. . . . When the first thrill of freedom subsides and anxiety rises to take its place, we begin to be tugged by that old yearning for safety, the wish to be saved.
— *Colette Rowling, writer*

Nancy's and Jan's stories demonstrate the truth in the old adage "Trust in God, but row away from the rocks." We can't afford to be naïve. We need to keep our eye on the details and not depend on corporations or spouses to take care of us.

Too many of us, born in the "Cinderella Generation," still believe that a handsome prince is going to ride in on a white horse and take care of us. In today's world, Cinderella's prince took off in search of himself, and the horse ran off with another woman!

As Gerry Laybourne, cofounder of the Oxygen Network and Oprah Winfrey's partner, told us, "It's your life, and you have to be responsible for all of it. It's not your husband's or lover's or partner's or best friend's or company's. You have to own it and live it."

Do you see yourself in Jan's or Nancy's story? If so, simply consider it a naïve mistake, extract the lesson, and move on, as both

Jan and Nancy have. There is no value in wallowing in what was done to you, no matter how unfair or undeserved. Resolve right now that you will move on.

Please know that many smart women have succumbed to the mistaken notion that "they will take care of me." Please take a few minutes to think through these questions before you answer them in your WIT Kit journal:

- Who do you believe is responsible for you?
- Do you own every aspect of your life?
- What nitty-gritty details have you left in the hands of others?

Then, write three things you will do to become more self-sufficient and less dependent on others.

15. Listen to your inner voice.

Follow your instincts. That's where true wisdom manifests itself.
— *Oprah Winfrey, television host (1954–)*

Nagging Doubts

Intuition is a natural consequence of self-esteem, the greatest power you can have. With it you broaden your life into an adventure, because you know in your gut that you can handle the unknown.
— *Caroline Myss, medical intuitive and writer*

Ignoring intuition, that tiny voice inside, is a mistake every woman we know has made. Here we are, equipped with one of the most powerful tools on the planet, and we don't listen to it. We don't listen until the intuitive voice reaches a crescendo we can no longer ignore.

Jackie has learned to trust that female voice inside. "In my first run for legislative office, I was not supported by those in power. As a result, I had to take out a loan against my townhouse to pay for a television commercial that we needed. I remember walking down the street with a copy of the signed promissory note in my hand and realizing the implications if I lost the election. Yet, this tiny voice inside me kept me strong. I knew that I had done the right thing. In an election where thousands of votes were cast, I won by a mere 400 votes!"

Kathryn Tunstall, chair of Conceptus Laboratories, refers to her intuition as "nagging doubts." Kathryn says that every time she has ignored her nagging doubts, she has lost time and money and relationships.

Michealene used to ignore that inner voice until it saved her from a possible mugging in the streets of Detroit. "I was walking downtown on my lunch break, when my intuition warned me something was amiss. The sun was shining and there were a lot of people on the street, so there should have been nothing to fear. Yet my inner warning system kept sending red alerts. I noticed two men watching me closely. One sat on the steps of a nearby building, and the other was walking directly toward me on the sidewalk. I began to run, looking directly at the man who was approaching me. I kept thinking if they caught me and assaulted me, at least I would be able to identify them. I also wanted them to know I wasn't going to be an easy target. Thankfully, I escaped, grateful for that inner voice that persisted until I paid attention."

"I think I realized the value of female intuition," says Deborah, "when one of the most successful businessmen in America told me that he made all of his big decisions with his heart and not his head. He told me that he had worked for years to develop his intuition, his gut, and his hunches. He had trained himself to call upon this skill in all large business decisions. When this corporate leader told me that he had worked for years to develop what I was born with," said Deborah, "I realized I was neglecting to use a part of my natural talent that could serve me a multitude of ways."

Your intuition can give you a competitive advantage in business and in life. It can serve as a warning system when you're at risk. It can also help you decide what to do when your flow of life turns into a tsunami. From now on, keep your antennae attuned to that small voice. When it speaks, listen and act accordingly. You won't regret following your intuition; you will only regret ignoring it.

16. Realize that risks are part of the package.

If you have made serious mistakes, there is always another chance for you. What we call failure is not the falling down, but the staying down.
　　—Mary Pickford, Canadian-born actress (1892–1979)

Wise Risks Are Worthwhile

If we could sell our experiences for what they cost us, we'd all be millionaires.
　　—Abigail Van Buren, newspaper columnist (1918–   )

Laura Lisawood, senior advisor at Goldman Sachs and secretary general of the United Nations Council on Women, interviewed thirteen women who were serving as heads of nations and countries. All thirteen told her, "Society does not tolerate women's mistakes as much as it does men's."

When you hear commentary like that from women leading nations, it doesn't take a rocket scientist to figure out why some women avoid taking risks!

Yet we cannot allow the arrows-in-the-back downside of being a pioneer stop us from forging ahead and taking risks. Our dear friend, Eunice Azzanni, partner at international search firm Korn Ferry, has a wonderful mantra for women to remember when deciding to take a risk. She says, "If you are not living on the edge, you are simply taking up too much room."

What is your attitude toward taking risks? Think back to a time you really stretched yourself and went after something. Did you start your own business even though there was a chance of financial failure? Did you try an adventure sport such as mountain climbing or skydiving? Did you go to a convention where you didn't know anyone? Did you dare to share an unpopular opinion at a staff meeting?

What was the outcome of that risk? Did it work out as you had hoped? What was your process for deciding whether that risk was wise or rash? Did you find that even if the risk didn't turn out perfectly, it was still worth it?

Write in your WIT Kit journal about a risk you're glad you took. Explain how it impacted you. Now, think of a risk you're considering. List all the possible consequences, good and bad. How could you benefit from taking this risk? How could you "lose"?

Make this risk you're contemplating the topic of your time during your next kitchen table group meeting. Get their opinions and check their input against your gut. If, after thinking this through, it seems like it's a wise risk, go for it. Understand that there are no guarantees that it will work out exactly the way you want, but know that you will derive many benefits simply from trying something new.

The WIT Kit
Exercises and Tools for Managing a Great Mistake

Champions keep playing until they get it right.
—Billie Jean King, Wimbledon tennis champ (1943–   )

1. How can you develop a scientific mind-set toward mistakes, to see them as "stepping-stones to success" rather than things to avoid or be ashamed of? Think about this question and then write your answer in your WIT Kit journal.

2. Make a list of three of your "best mistakes" in your WIT Kit journal. What are three things that went wrong, that you regretted doing or not doing, or that didn't turn out the way you wanted them to?

3. What did you learn from those mistakes? How are you actually better off now because of the valuable lessons you learned?

4. Finish this sentence: "From now on when I make a mistake, I'm going to _____."

5. There is an important rule for this exercise: you must promise yourself that you will not get depressed over your mistakes and wallow in sorrow. Look at your mistakes for clues and insights that will allow you to move forward, not backward.

6. Make the topic of your next kitchen table group "The Best Mistakes We've Made." Acknowledge your top three mistakes

in life and describe what you learned from each mistake. Be sure to have your WIT Kit journal with you so you can record important insights.

chapter three

Make Courage an Everyday Companion

17. Know it's the obstacles in the stream that make it sing.

I want to know if you can get up after the night of grief and despair, weary and bruised to the bone, and do what needs to be done to feed the children.
—*Oriah Mountain Dreamer, writer*

Courage Needs a Partner
A woman is like a tea bag. It's only when she is in hot water that you realize how strong she is.
—*Nancy Reagan, former first lady (1921–   )*

"She was a tenured professor living with an accomplished doctor in the suburbs," says Deborah. "When I first met her, I remember thinking how lucky she was. Brilliant, beautiful, and wealthy, my friend had the perfect life. What I did not know was that inside of her lovely two-story home in the suburbs, a nightmare played out each night. Her husband beat her, threatened her, and in his drug-induced paranoia, made her believe that if she ever left him, he would have her killed.

"One day, mustering up every ounce of courage she could find, she simply left. She took a bag of makeup, a book, and $500 in cash with no plan other than to free herself from a bad situation. She bought a one-way train ticket to the east coast and moved in with an old friend. Today, twenty years later, she is a happy and confident woman, a well-known author, and a celebrated educator. She always comes to mind," says Deborah, "when I think of the word *courage.*"

Courage. It stems from the French word *coeur,* which means "heart." Leave it to the French to uncover the secret that deep within our hearts we will find the willpower and tenacity to face and embrace life's hardships. The esteemed psychologist Rollo May said, "Just as one's heart helps our body to function, pumping blood to our physical organs, courage makes possible all the virtues of human kind. Without courage, we have no real and authentic life."

Courage is as essential to a "survive and thrive" lifestyle as water is to a fish. Without a reservoir of courage to call upon, we become wearied and beaten by life's inevitable challenges. Courage must always have a partner—a crisis or a seemingly insurmountable problem. It waits patiently for that obstacle with which to partner so it might be unleashed in all its glory.

"MY WORLD'S COLLAPSING, YET SOMEHOW I MUSTER THE WILL TO EAT CHOCOLATE."

Many think of the word *courage* only as defined in the dictionary: "perseverance, moral and mental strength, facing fear and failure or overcoming difficulty and obstacles," and see it solely as a solitary journey. We believe the journey of courage is best walked with women friends who, literally and figuratively, "en-courage" us.

In the pages that follow, we share the stories of some very courageous women. We hope their moving stories will help you develop the courage you need to deal with the challenges you face, now and in the future. One of the many beautiful aspects of courage is that it's contagious. The more you choose to act in spite of your fear, the easier it is to do.

18. Realize that courage often means letting go.

Nothing in life is to be feared. It is only to be understood.
—*Madame Marie Curie, Polish-born chemist (1867–1934)*

Holding On at All Costs
Life shrinks or expands in proportion to one's courage.
—*Anaïs Nin, French writer (1903–1977)*

Michealene had a gifted acting coach early in her career. Having taught many famous actors, he had the ability to help people discover untapped skills and strengths residing deep inside. At the start of each class, he would have his students close their eyes and run through a series of deep-breathing exercises. Each class member would say something aloud, and the coach would repeat it, like a mantra.

"'It is so hard to let go,' Michealene blurted out. Much to her embarrassment, the coach stopped the class. He asked the students to open their eyes and, while looking directly at her, said, 'It is not hard to let go. It is more difficult to hold on. Imagine the cat holding on to a limb of a tree. The longer it holds on, the heavier its body becomes. What is hard is continuing to have the strength to hold on.'

"In that moment I realized I had to change my definition of courage. Backward, I had it all backward. Holding on to everything at all costs was what I had defined as strength. Yet I realized that letting go was the truly courageous act."

Letting go played a role in Suki Forbes Bigham's act of courage. Suki lived a charmed life, with a successful husband, a prominent career in the biotechnology field, and three beautiful children—Cabot, age eight; Charlotte, age six; and Beatrice, age three. They were living the California dream, but they could not ignore the pull of family in Boston, so they returned to the East. Her elder daughter, Charlotte, suffered from high fevers, but other than sleepless nights, it was not of serious concern. Yet over the summer, Suki noticed Charlotte becoming very muscular, like a gymnast, for no apparent reason. Her sister-in-law, a nurse, suspected that Charlotte suffered from malignant hyperthermia, a condition in which the body is unable to cool itself down.

One August day when Charlotte wasn't feeling well, Suki, on instinct, took her to the local hospital. By the time they arrived, Charlotte's fever was 102. The doctor was hesitant to admit Charlotte—fevers of 102 were common—but Suki demanded that they take Charlotte and expressed her fear of malignant hyperthermia. Charlotte's fever continued to climb, and when it hit 108 degrees, she went into cardiac arrest. The doctors could not revive her. Charlotte, a beautiful six-year-old full of life, arrived at noon and was pronounced dead at 3 P.M.

In three short hours, Suki Forbes Bigham's charmed life had been shattered. Suki told us, "When one suffers a great loss, the option pool for the next step is pretty grim. I saw three choices: (1) choose to die, (2) choose to exist until I die, or (3) choose to live. Option 3 was the most difficult, but frankly it was the only option available. There is always a choice. I want women to remember that there is always a choice, and it resides within us to choose."

Positive Attitudes Are Underrated

A strong, positive mental attitude will create more miracles than any wonder drug.
    —Patricia Neal, actress (1926–)

"Losing Charlotte has been the most devastating experience of my forty years," said Suki. "I expect it to be the most devastating experience of my next forty. Since I can't wish my little girl back to life, I want to pull some lessons from her short life. When I see her again, I want to be able to tell her how profoundly her loss affected me—not in the negative and obvious ways, but in the ways that have made me a better person; in the ways that I hope to help other people; in the ways that I hope I am able to bring some of her gentle, impish spirit into all that I do while I remain here.

"Grief is a delicate dance," Suki states. "It is two steps forward, two steps back, and then sometimes a huge dip. The process of letting go is healing, yet it requires something difficult when love is involved. It is easy to be surrounded by and utterly immersed in the pain of loss. That fullness keeps the loss very present. The hard part is letting go of some of the weight and still feeling connected. I have not mastered that, and I don't know if I ever want to. All I know is that the next forty-plus years, the time I need to wait until I see my daughter again, will go by much more quickly if I can somehow find a way to get back into life. To find joy. To stay vital and to stay in love with possibilities.

"Positive attitudes are underrated. Without one, I would still be in bed right now. Some days it comes easier than others, but I am determined. I owe it to my surviving children, to my husband, to Charlotte, to myself. The hardest part in the process was 'letting go' of the grief so I could be fully available to help my children and my husband get through their own grief."

Are you in the middle of a heartbreaking situation where the real act of courage is letting go of grief, resentment, or anger? What is that situation? What are the consequences of hanging on? What are the benefits of moving on?

19. Develop a funny bone.

It is better to be a lion for a day than a sheep all of your life.
    —Elizabeth Kenny, Australian nurse (1880–1952)

Stressed Is Desserts Spelled Backward
Reality is something you rise above.
    —Liza Minnelli, actress (1946–   )

Saranne Rothberg sat on the bed in the New York hotel room and laughed, sharing with Michealene some of the corny jokes she and her daughter Lauriel had always exchanged. "As we continued to share these corny jokes," Michealene said, "we could not stop laughing. Suddenly, Saranne's laugh turned strange, almost a half-laugh, half-cry from some cavernous well deep inside her. The tears came gushing forth as she grieved for the unfairness for her daughter and the regrets she had about her own life. Then, she became quiet. When she looked at me, I realized that, in that moment, she had switched from focusing on the past to looking ahead to the future."

In February 1999, Saranne had heard those dreaded words: *malignant tumor, breast cancer, surgery, radiation, chemo,* and she felt as if she had forgotten how to breathe.

Saranne said, "The medical staff continued to banter about the prognosis for my exposed breasts when suddenly my mind rebelled. I'd read a magazine article about Norman Cousins, who had 'laughed himself well.' In the middle of my diagnosis, that article hijacked my thoughts. The diagnosing doctor had just informed me it was too late on a Friday to assemble their hospital cancer squad. With that, and with what I readily admit might have been a slightly hysterical reaction, I yanked off my hospital gown and ran from the Englewood Breast Center to the local video store in search of comedy tapes.

THELMA TAKES HER ANXIETIES
TO THE STREETS.

"In the video store, I was like an emotional grand canyon of fear, anxiety, and depression. If laughing had helped Norman Cousins heal his rare nerve disease two decades ago, why couldn't I amuse my cancer for sixty hours? What did I have to lose? Armed with stacks of stand-up comedy performances and feature films, I returned home still reeling from the logistics of what it meant to fight cancer. I wooed my five-year-old daughter to her bed earlier than usual.

"I was barely holding back a flood of tears as we said our prayers. Torturous questions bombarded my mind: 'How many more bedtime stories will I read to her? Will I be strong enough to bathe her after chemo starts?' Sobbing, I ran to the television in the other room and fumbled to insert the first videotape. Could the comedy cavalry rescue me the way Norman Cousins had documented in his article?"

Lighten Up Instead of Tighten Up
Laughter rises out of tragedy when you need it the most and rewards you for your courage.
—*Erma Bombeck, humorist and writer (1927–1996)*

"I sat in front of the monitor, praying for a miracle. A young Eddie Murphy appeared on the screen, set up his first joke, delivered the punch line, and the audience's laughter filled my room. I demanded that my mind listen to Eddie even though it was more interested in self-chatter about my own mortality. Another Murphy joke, I laughed and blew my nose. Another joke, I laughed and cried. Another joke, more guffaws from deep inside. I could still laugh! I realized the cancer that was ravaging my healthy breast tissue couldn't rob me of my ability to laugh unless I let it. I switched to a Jackie Mason video. With each laugh came a deeper breath. With each deeper breath came relaxation. With relaxation came a sense of welcomed calm. I was now laughing multiple times per minute, and life seemed manageable again.

"As the east coast went to sleep, Robin Williams's genius caused me to laugh without pause. His manic antics jiggled all those stomach knots caused by the cancer diagnosis. Next, my cancerous left breast and I started laughing at Jerry Seinfeld's 'Lost Socks in the Dryer' monologue. I slapped my knees in shared mirth—I lose half a pair every time I do laundry too.

"Then, it hit me. I am not alone. Millions of people are going through this cancer journey too. We're supposed to connect. Like everyone else diagnosed with a life-threatening illness, I was stressed. But with the help of Norman Cousins and a myriad of other comics, I received a crash course in comic perspective. Their humorous outlook on life instilled in me the determination to continue to laugh even while undergoing my dark nights of the soul.

"It's been almost five years, three surgeries, forty-four radiation treatments, and too many chemo cocktails since my all-night comedy marathon. I am now considered cancer-free. And at least twice a day I connect with comedy as a tribute to Norman Cousins and all the comics who have given me my life's mission at the ComedyCures Foundation. From its grassroots launch during my first chemo treatment, it became clear that I had been given a unique opportunity to bring joy and humor to others through this nonprofit service. And the punch line: my funny bone, once fractured, is now healed." Visit *www.comedycures.com* to learn more about what Saranne and her sidekicks at Comedy Cures are up to.

How do you keep your sense of humor when things aren't going your way? Fun is not frivolous. Keeping your "wit" about you is vital to maintaining a positive perspective in the midst of negative events.

Why not post your favorite cartoons and funny quotes where you can see them all the time? It's a way to feed your funny bone on a daily basis, to lighten up instead of tighten up.

20. Walk through fields of fear.

Not truth, but faith, it is that keeps the world alive.
— Edna St. Vincent Millay, poet (1892–1950)

The Killing Fields
The soul can split the sky in two and let the face of God shine through.
— Edna St. Vincent Millay, poet (1892–1950)

Letting go of fear opens up space for courage to come into our lives. Yet fear can be one of the most difficult obstacles to overcome as a woman struggles to rise to the surface in a life that keeps dragging her down.

Whenever the four of us of become fearful, we think of Vornida Seng. In our opinion, there is no more powerful story, no more potent antidote to fear, than Vornida Seng's personal journey.

Thirty years ago, Vornida Seng walked for weeks across her native Cambodia. Today, the memories still haunt her—memories of her ten-year-old brother's cries during the torture he received for stealing fruit. She hears the screams of her brothers and sisters as soldiers dump their mother's body into an unmarked grave. As the sole surviving member of her family's tragic demise in the killing fields of Cambodia, not one day passes that she does not remember each of her four siblings who died in her arms.

Today, hope lives for Vornida in her two American-born children. Someday she will tell her children what happened to her. And the story she will tell begins when Khmer Rouge soldiers burst into the five-bedroom home of Vornida and her family.

Vietnamese dictator Pol Pot had decided that in order to create the perfect communist state, he would first empty the cities of Cambodia. "Thousands of people filled the streets," Vornida recalls. "Corpses lay by the road. Hospital patients, some with IV bottles, tried to walk with the crowd. I began to walk, and I walked for weeks," she recounted. "We reached a village near the Thailand border. I was eleven at the time, and I, along with my mother and siblings, were forced to work twelve hours a day in the rice fields."

They built their own primitive hut from the surrounding bamboo trees. Vornida's grandmother and sister contracted malaria, and within days her grandmother was dead. Three weeks later, Vornida's little sister, her eyes open and full of tears, died in her lap. Vornida's mother, like most of the villagers, was starving. She died and left Vornida to care for her remaining siblings. "We ate anything," she recalls, "from scorpions to lizards, rats, and grasshoppers." Vornida and her brothers Siphano, nine, and Visothy, eight, and her sister Methegany, ten, were sent to a mountain prison camp. Visothy died in Vornida's arms of high fever and starvation. Soldiers tied little Siphano to a tree. "His eyes were shut, and the soldiers kept hitting him with their rifles. They brought bees and ants to sting him until he lost consciousness." He died shortly thereafter.

In December 1978, the Pol Pot regime started to crumble. Carrying her remaining sister, Methegany, in a basket, Vornida started to walk again. She walked hundreds of miles to a neighboring village and hitched a ride to the province of Siem Reap in frantic search of a hospital for little Methegany. A few days later, Methegany died.

With the death of the last of her siblings, Vornida believed her "life and . . . dreams were over." A local driver for *Time* magazine took her in and alerted the Bangkok bureau chief. *Time* magazine sponsored Vornida, paid her passage to the United States, and gave her the job she continues to hold today in New York City. Vornida Seng believes that God meant for her to survive for a reason. When she looks into the eyes of her two small children, she says, "My family lives on in them."

The next time you feel fear creeping into your life, remember the inspirational story of Vornida Seng. Fear did not stop Vornida as she made her way across her native country. Fear did not prevent Vornida from building a new life, from finding love, or from starting a family again in her new world. Vornida could have easily chosen to live the rest of her life in denial or depression. Who could have blamed her? Yet she did not. Vornida kept walking through life, one foot in front of the other. She chose to believe that the suffering she and her family had experienced could serve some higher purpose. Vornida Seng is a living, breathing testimony to what we can do if we choose to persevere through pain and walk through fear.

Learning to Walk through Fear

Even in the darkest phase, be it thick or thin, always someone marches brave here beneath my skin.

—k.d. lang, singer and writer (1961—   )

Have you been devastated by a tragedy? Are you mourning the loss of a loved one? Has something happened to you or someone close to you that is deeply unfair? Are you fearful of the future?

Putting one foot in front of another, one step at a time, one day at a time, will bring you closer to a life that is once again full of love, health, and contribution. When Vornida was working in the rice fields, starving in a mountain prison camp, and fleeing her country by foot, she had no way of knowing that one day she would be gifted with two healthy children, a satisfying job, and her own home.

Stories like Vornida's can inspire you to keep walking. Vornida is proof of the tenacity of the human spirit, its ability to transcend fears and tragic circumstances. When you feel fear percolating up into your life, visualize Vornida Seng walking beside you as you begin to take your own steps forward.

21. Be brave on your own behalf.

When you get to the end of your rope, tie a knot in it and hang on.
    —*Eleanor Roosevelt, former first lady (1884–1962)*

The Mom from Petaluma
*Courage is the price that life exacts for granting peace. The soul that
knows it not knows no release from little things.*
    —*Amelia Earhart, aviator (1897–1937)*

Courageous acts can consist of righting a wrong, facing a situation
that seems overwhelming, or not backing down from a bully. When
we first met Denise Garibaldi, she was a soft-spoken woman from
a small town. Denise found her courage as a result of a tragedy that
took the life of her teenaged son.

This mom from Petaluma, California, touched the nation with
her poignant testimony to Congress in what became a historic
congressional hearing on anabolic steroids and their increasing use by
high school, college, and professional athletes. Sitting directly behind
such baseball legends as Sammy Sosa and Jose Canseco during the
House Government Reform Committee hearings, Denise witnessed
one major league baseball player after another refuse to discuss, or
outright deny, allegations that they had used steroids.

Why was Denise at the hearing? Three years earlier, her son Rob
had committed suicide as a result of a deep depression brought on
by his steroid use. As a senior in high school he had been a gifted
baseball player; he had been drafted by the New York Yankees, but he
had chosen instead to accept a scholarship to play for the University
of Southern California.

Spurred on by coaches and trainers who told him he needed
to "get bigger in order to become better," Rob turned to anabolic

steroids. He defended his actions by telling his parents, "This is what all professional baseball players do." He said, "Mom, these are not drugs. They're supplements, and all the major league players use them." He backed up his claim by naming several well-known athletes who had admitted in TV interviews they used these "harmless" supplements. Denise struggled to save her son, placing him in rehabilitation clinics and arranging for private therapy. Unfortunately, she could not wrestle him away from the drug's powerful grip and its damaging effects.

After Rob's death, Denise began to speak out about the trainers and coaches who she believed contributed to her son's death by issuing their daily mantra of "get bigger or get beaten." Many tried to intimidate her into silence, threatening her with lawsuits. But her courage grew threefold, and she joined forces with other parents who were coming forward to tell their own heartbreaking stories.

A Mom on a Mission
Mothers are the pivot on which the whole world spins.
  —*Pam Brown, writer and poet (1948—   )*

In less than a year, we witnessed Denise garner a worldwide audience for her important message. Denise had become a "mom on a mission," and history shows that such moms have been changing the world for a very long time. Denise, who otherwise would never have sought a national spotlight, told us the day before her congressional testimony that she derived her courage from her hope that Rob's life and death would not be forgotten. Her goal was to alert parents to the dangers of steroids to save them and their families from the pain and loss she had experienced.

She said, "It is also my time to tell our national heroes, the ones our children look up to, that players who take steroids and other performance-enhancing drugs are not only cheaters, but cowards.

I want them to stand up and be counted. I want them to show our children a different way to compete at the top levels so we can put an end to this madness. They hide behind their unions with the help of management and powerfully connected people. Too many famous athletes and sports teams have resisted facing this issue. How many more Robs are out there trying to emulate their heroes, not knowing this path can lead to their early death?"

Rock the Boat

Mother love is the fuel that enables a normal human being to do the impossible.
— *Marion C. Garretty, writer (1917—   )*

Is there something going on around you that is not right? Are you afraid to voice your concerns because you were taught not to rock the boat? Do you consider yourself shy, timid, or soft-spoken? That didn't stop Denise. We're not suggesting you be rash, but we are suggesting that silence changes nothing. If you feel strongly that something you're witnessing is wrong, then you have a responsibility to bring it to the attention of whoever is in a position to do something about it. All of us have had to confront an individual or organization that "wronged" us. It wasn't easy. Yet we all are glad we didn't suffer in silence and allow the inappropriate situation to continue.

22. Earn your own red badge of courage.

Character contributes to beauty. It fortifies a woman. Her mode of conduct, a standard of courage, discipline, fortitude, and integrity, can do a great deal to make a woman beautiful.
— *Jacqueline Bisset, model and actress (1944—   )*

The Steely Look of Resolve

Each of us brings to our jobs, whatever it is, our lifetime of experiences and our values and our courage.

— *Sandra Day O'Connor, first woman Supreme Court Justice*
(1930–)

"Twenty years ago," Deborah said, "we had bumper stickers created for one of Jackie's political campaigns that read, 'The Courage to Lead.' That slogan reminds me on a daily basis of the inspiration I've received from knowing her. If there really were a red badge of courage, I would give it to my friend Jackie Speier. Firsthand, I've witnessed her call upon her courage in one challenging situation after another.

"I was with Jackie, in the hospital, the day she had to decide to take her husband off life support. Three months pregnant at the time, and in the midst of devastating grief, Jackie focused on the best way to break the news to Jackson, her five-year-old son. After the funeral, I sat next to her on the sofa in her living room. Newly widowed, she was also six weeks away from impending bankruptcy. The pain I felt for her that day was overwhelming, yet Jackie remained focused on the options available to her. She endured.

"Fast forward to six months later, from the sofa in her living room to the hospital delivery room: I was gathered with a group of friends as Jackie gave birth to Stephanie, her second child. I couldn't imagine what it must have been like to give birth only six months after burying a husband. However, I witnessed the steely look of resolve in Jackie's eyes. Over the years, I've become accustomed to that 'look,' and when I see it, I know Jackie's headed for another red badge of courage!

"One time I sat next to Jackie at an awards dinner. I was the only one in the audience who knew that Jackie was wearing a bulletproof vest. Her life had been threatened because she was attempting to pass legislation in the state of California that would sanction an absent father's wages if he was in arrears on child support payments. In the restroom, before the awards dinner began, Jackie ripped open her blouse to show me the bulletproof vest. We both agreed that it added extra inches to her cleavage, but it was a heck of a way to a better figure! Thankfully, the awards dinner drew to a conclusion with no unpleasant surprises.

"Several years later, I saw Jackie squarely face the financial and banking industry in a high-stakes endeavor to pass a privacy bill that protected Californians' personal and financial information. Astoundingly, nearly $20 million in special interest funds rolled into Sacramento, California, into the pockets of lawyers, lobbying groups, and industry veterans. They were all aimed directly at derailing Jackie Speier. During the evening news that night, I saw Jackie on television. I saw that look in Jackie's eyes. I knew at that precise moment that $20 million and a well-connected contingency of bankers, lawyers, and lobbyists were not a match for my friend Jackie."

Courage in Everyday Life

Do not let your fire go out, spark by irreplaceable spark, in the hopeless swamps of the approximate, the not-quite, the not-yet, the not-at-all. Do not let the hero in your soul perish, in lonely frustration for the life you deserved, but have never been able to reach.

—*Ayn Rand, Russian-born novelist and philosopher (1905–1982)*

The steely look of resolve in Jackie's eyes resurfaced once again last year after she had decided to speak out on corruption and inefficiencies in the California state prison system. The powerful California Correctional Peace Officers Association (CCPOA), a union composed of prison guards, targeted her in a series of public relations ploys. They organized a large rally at Raley Field in Sacramento, where more than 5,000 people gathered. From the podium, leaders of the CCPOA painted Jackie Speier as their enemy. On the streets of Sacramento, these same people handed out phony dollar bills that carried derogatory statements about her. Yet they could not see what I saw.

Behind the enormous desk in her Senate chambers, I viewed the silhouette of the woman I have known for most of my adult life. She looked so small. After all, she stands 5 feet, 4 $^1/_2$ inches tall and, even on a day when she and her staff have binged on chocolate, she might weigh in at 130 pounds. Yet when her eyes met mine, I knew the CCPOA had met their match in the petite, feminine, and unflinchingly strong Jackie Speier.

Several days later, I had a serious discussion with Jackie. I was quite worried about her and felt that she was not being strategic enough in her approach to the prison situation in California. She looked at me and told me something I will always remember. She said, "Deborah, after my life experiences I have nothing left to fear. Where I see wrong, I will do my best to make it right, no matter the cost. The worst thing that can happen is that I'll lose an election. That does not seem like a very big price to pay considering what I have already lived through."

Jackie is a testimony to the fact that courage can be and should be our everyday companion. When I am feeling intimidated, I think of her. Her example always motivates me to move forward instead of shrinking back and wilting in defeat.

Who is your shining example? Whom do you admire as a walking, talking role model of courage? Is it your mom, Mahatma Gandhi, your sister, aunt, Eleanor Roosevelt, or a woman business owner? Is it a neighbor who participates in the March against Breast Cancer each year?

What is it about that person that causes you to respect her or him? Can you think of a specific situation in which she held her head high and forged ahead despite daunting circumstances? In your WIT Kit journal, describe what happened and the choice he made to face his fears rather than flee from them.

What challenging situation are you facing? How would your role model handle it? Could you learn from his or her behavior so you can handle your own circumstances with more confidence? Plan exactly what you are going to say and do so you can resolve that situation with courage.

23. Let yourself cry when Tinkerbell dies.

Love has pride in nothing—but its own humility.
    —Clare Booth Luce, congresswoman and diplomat (1903–1987)

The Courage to Stay
I realized that if what we call human nature can be changed, then absolutely anything is possible. From that moment my life changed.
    —Shirley MacLaine, actress (1934—   )

Courage can appear as cowardice from the outside—until one looks more closely.

Two of us have experienced infidelity in our marriages. One husband took a mistress, while another husband took several! As always, we turned to our friends for advice and comfort. Some thought we should immediately divorce, dumping the jerks and bidding farewell. One friend entertained the thought that quite possibly our marriages could be saved if we could call forth the courage to stay.

"When I found out about my husband's affair, I remember feeling so alone. I was devastated by his infidelity. I felt like Tinkerbell, believing that the world was wonderful while living with a man like Peter Pan, who I hoped would eventually grow up. I remember quite clearly the day I realized I was living a 'make-believe' life. Pregnant at the time, I went to get an AIDS test because my husband had confessed to an affair. Not only had my husband committed adultery, he had had unprotected sex that put our child and me at risk.

"As I sat in the hallway of that tiny laboratory waiting for my test, I shared my secret with the nurse. Surprisingly, she told me that I was the third pregnant and married woman that week to come in for the same reason. Gee, I thought, maybe I should start a club!

"HONEY, I'M RUNNING OUT FOR 30 OR 40 YEARS.
THERE'S FOOD IN THE FRIDGE."

"Every book I read and every story I heard depicted expectant parents as happy and full of anticipation. Here I was, very expectant but unhappy and miserable. I was up and down, never knowing from one minute to the next what I was going to do, think, or feel. One day I was leaving. The next day I was kicking him out of our home. Add to the equation my rampant hormones from the pregnancy, and I was a walking, talking basket case.

"I remembered another woman who had had to deal with the infidelity of her husband, who just happened to be president of the United States. She had had to endure this very personal betrayal in public. I read letters in the *New York Times* editorial section, where complete strangers took it upon themselves to criticize her for staying with her husband. Versions of Tammy Wynette's 'Stand by Your Man' played incessantly on the radio. Yet, I knew that the choice she made required an extreme act of courage.

"I've come to believe it takes as much courage to stay in a relationship and face pain, anger, and betrayal as it does to leave. After I made the decision to stay, it took two years of heartbreaking and excruciating work to repair our marriage. Rebuilding trust with someone who has been unfaithful and learning to forgive that person sometimes seemed harder than getting a divorce.

"Today, I have a strong relationship with my husband, better than at any point in our marriage. He is a conscious, loving father. Quite surprisingly, he is now everything I have always wanted him to be. He became an adult man, fully responsible for his actions and their effects upon others. He almost lost his family, but through the pain we gained so much more.

"Looking back, I now know his affair was his own journey into courage. Although we've had a happy ending, the sadness over what happened didn't just disappear. Tinkerbell no longer lives in my heart. She exited for Neverland; however, in her wake she left the mature, 'real-life' marriage that my husband and I now share."

Are You Tinkerbell?

Remember that people come and go, and of all the people in your life, you are the one who is there to stay. You are the one who can choose to love yourself, choose to respect yourself, and promise with all your heart and soul that you will never leave you.

—Kimberly Kirberger, writer

Courage is doing what's right for you. Many women show incredible courage by leaving bad marriages and abusive relationships. Others feel the more courageous act is to stay and try to make them better. Only you can decide what's best for you. The point is to make a conscious choice about your plan of action rather than bowing to pressure or pretending that everything is just fine.

Are you in a relationship? How would you describe it? If it's everything you want it to be, congratulations. If the other person is not treating you with the love or respect you want or deserve, what are you going to do about it?

Are you going to sit down with that person and discuss your concerns and articulate how you both can treat each other better? Are you going to suggest the two of you see a counselor together? If your safety is in jeopardy, are you going to pack your bags and head to the opposite end of the country?

Whatever you do, please call up the courage to do something rather nothing. Be brave on your own behalf rather than passively enduring the pain of a relationship where your needs are not being met or you are being violated.

24. Wear a courage bracelet.

Don't get hung up on a snag in the stream. Snags alone are not dangerous; it's the debris that clings to them that makes the trouble. Pull yourself loose and go on.
    —Anne Shannon Moore, writer and lecturer

The Sweaty Palms of Courage
I've been absolutely terrified every moment of my life—and I've never let it keep me from doing a single thing I wanted to do.
    —Georgia O'Keeffe, artist (1887–1986)

Deborah's friend Gary Heil wears a wristband given to him by Jim Brogan, a famous basketball player. On the wristband are three words: Goals, Attitude, and Courage. Those words serve as a constant reminder to reflect on these questions:

- Am I clear about what I want to accomplish?
- Am I clear about who I am?
- Do I have the courage to be authentic even when it is tough?
- Do I have the courage to commit to the truth and do the right thing, not the expeditious thing?
- Am I positive and optimistic even in the face of failure?

Deborah witnessed the profound impact these questions had on her friend's behavior. The change in his interactions with others was nothing short of remarkable. Deborah decided to make her own bracelet. She went to her favorite department store and bought a leather strap and seven crystal letter charms, spelling out the word *courage.*

"Looking at the word *courage* each day has had a powerful effect upon me. The bracelet reminds me to be authentic in times of difficulty, to tell the truth even when it hurts, to be confident in my choices, and to remember that courage is within me waiting to be called upon. It may sound simplistic, but if I find myself in an uncomfortable situation, I just look at the word *courage* and it gives me strength I didn't feel a moment before."

Don't Sit in the Audience of Life

And then the day came when the risk to remain tight in a bud was more painful than the risk it took to blossom.

—Anaïs Nin, French writer (1903–1977)

In our discussions with women about the roadblocks they face, we noticed that three consistent themes tended to permeate women's stories: fear, denial, and self-sabotage.

Fear expresses itself in many ways, from sweaty palms to full-blown anxiety attacks. We have also seen fear used as a crutch. We all have known women who point to their bosses, friends, spouses, or kids as the reason they were not living the life they dreamed of. "He intimidates me." "She is threatened by me." "He will leave me if I make more money than him." "They demand too much of me." These thoughts and feelings can manifest as fears that are used as an emotional shield to hide behind.

Denial can help us avoid feelings of abandonment, loss, and loss of intimacy. Like an old bathrobe melding perfectly to our bodies, denial comforts us. It's important not to be deceived by its comfort, however, because denial keeps us from leading an authentic life. Denial is the antithesis of courage.

Don't Dance with Self-Sabotage

Greatness is not measured by what a woman accomplishes, but by the
opposition she has had to overcome to reach her goals.
    — *Dorothy Heights, civil rights activist (1912–   )*

Unfortunately, another all-too-common pattern we've seen among women is the dance of self-sabotage. This is a dirty little trick that women use to mask their insecurities. Self-sabotage can be as simple as downplaying compliments. It can be as complex as not showing up for a job interview because "they weren't going to hire me anyway."

There are many reasons women do this, but more often than not it is a way to subconsciously derail ourselves on the path to where we want to go or what we want to do. As one woman told us, "Sitting in the audience can be easier than taking center stage. It takes a great deal of courage to go from being part of the crowd to being in front of the crowd."

We owe it to ourselves and all those we care about to willingly and eagerly take center stage. We believe taking center stage was what Marianne Williamson meant when she said, "Our deepest fear is not that we are inadequate. Our deepest fear is that we are power-ful beyond measure. It is our light, not our darkness, that frightens us. We ask ourselves, 'Who am I to be brilliant, gorgeous, talented, fabulous?' Actually, who are you *not* to be? There's nothing enlight-ened about shrinking so that other people won't feel insecure around you.... It's not just in some of us; it's in everyone. And as we let our own light shine, we unconsciously give other people permission to do the same. As we're liberated from our own fear, our presence automatically liberates others."

Do you downplay your talents? Have you been taught not to be conceited and found you've gone to the other extreme—being

overly self-effacing? Are you a perfectionist who never seems to live up to your very high standards? Do you belittle yourself?

All of these are subtle forms of self-sabotage. We're not suggesting you become egotistical. It's healthy to understand that we have something to offer and to take responsibility for giving our gifts to the world. Humility taken to an extreme becomes a weakness. As Marianne Williamson stated so eloquently, thinking small helps no one.

What are your skills, talents, and strengths? How are you going to capitalize on those so you can contribute more to the world? Instead of doubting your value, how are you going to have faith in yourself? What is something you want to try? How are you going to talk yourself into giving it a try? Perhaps you can begin by designing your own *courage* bracelet and wearing it every day. When those fears or self-sabotaging worries start creeping in, look at your bracelet and remind yourself that doubts never accomplished anything of value; only action can add value to you and those around you.

25. Know that courage isn't only owned by heroes.

Courage is more exhilarating than fear, and it is easier. Meeting each thing that comes up. Seeing it not as dreadful as it appeared but discovering that we have the strength to stare it down.
— *Eleanor Roosevelt, former first lady (1884–1962)*

Courage Doesn't Always Roar

There are some things you learn best in calm, and some in storm.
— *Willa Cather, writer (1873–1947)*

Courage can save lives, tell public truths, and help one face life-altering situations. Yet courage does not have to be played out on a national stage. As Mary Anne Radmacher, who coined the phrase, says, "courage doesn't always roar. Sometimes courage is the quiet voice at the end of the day saying, 'I will try again tomorrow.'"

Cindy Solomon coaches and trains executives to have more courage and take more risks. "It all began when I would speak at corporate meetings and women would line up to talk to me afterward. Many would tell me what great 'courage' I had for starting my own company and being on the lecture circuit. I certainly didn't see myself as being courageous, but I kept hearing the same refrain. After talking to hundreds of executives, I began to study this fascinating concept. Through my research, I realized that people rarely feel they deserve the label 'courageous' for doing something that seems natural or that comes easily to them.

"I concluded that courage is a highly individualized act. It is why we can perceive other people as being courageous when they haven't a clue they did anything out of the ordinary. I realized that while it's the bigger-than-life examples of courage that grab the headlines, courage is not the exclusive territory of 'heroes.' It is a compilation of the everyday moments of our lives, when we choose to do what's right rather than what's easy. I tell executives, 'Courage doesn't always roar. Sometimes courage is the quiet voice at the end of the day saying, "I will try again tomorrow."' For many people, this is how they learn to become braver on their own behalf."

Philosopher Ruth Gordon says it best: "Courage is like a muscle, strengthened by its use." We women need to give ourselves credit for the things we do each day that are courageous—deciding to propose an idea in a meeting, asking for a well-deserved raise, holding a colleague accountable for an unfulfilled commitment—each time we face facts instead of running from them, we build our courage muscle.

Creating courage is akin to taking up a new sport. We can't expect to run the Boston Marathon if we haven't trained for it. We won't play perfect tennis the first time we pick up a racquet. If we persevere through the discomfort of trying something new, we can become more confident about standing up for ourselves.

Radha Basu is yet another example of someone who learned to be brave on her own behalf. Radha always wanted to be an engineer. She was born in Chennai, in southern India, and ancient tradition demanded that she marry and become a homemaker. Radha had a different dream for herself. Her father's disapproval of Radha's dream was the first mountain Radha would need to scale.

Learn to "Trek"

We must believe that we are gifted for something, and that this thing, at whatever cost, must be attained.

—Madame Marie Curie, Polish-born chemist (1867–1934)

Radha secretly applied to engineering school and was a stellar candidate. Her father was furious, and it took courage for Radha, at a young age, to stand up to her culture and her father. "I have a view that you fight for the 20 percent that you feel very strongly about. Don't go to bat for every single thing. You pick your 20 percent and you be sure of your position and you fight hard," said Radha.

In 1972, she set out for the United States, alone and against her parents' wishes. She continued her studies and received a master's degree in electronics and computer engineering. It was 1974, and one could count on both hands the number of women engineers in Silicon Valley. Radha was now one of them. Hired as a research scientist at Hewlett-Packard, Radha rose through the ranks. "The first HP office in India began around my family's dining room table in New Delhi," said Radha. Working for another decade with Hewlett-Packard, Radha added marriage and the birth of her daughter to her full life. In late 1998, she scaled the next large mountain in her life—Mount Everest.

She and her husband hiked up 18,000 feet in their first trek together. "It was a physical, emotional, and spiritual journey," Radha said. "You learn in mountain trekking that when you think you can't take another step, you realize a car is not going to magically appear to drive you down the mountain. If I decided to go forward, I would need to trek. If I decided to go down the mountain, I would need to trek. Either way, I was on the journey, so I chose to go forward."

Not only did Radha scale Mount Everest, but upon her return she resigned from Hewlett-Packard and started her own technology company, taking it public in 2001. As a female chief executive officer of South Asian descent, Radha has encountered more than her share of discrimination. She views these issues as simply another mountain to climb. "If I am being discriminated against, most of the time I don't even notice it. If there is a glass ceiling, I shall kick it in. Do whatever one has to do, but don't imagine it's there. Just keep scaling the mountain and keep moving forward. Don't let others' prejudices be used to limit you."

Have you been discriminated against? Have you allowed peoples' prejudices to hold you back from achieving what you wanted or deserved? How can you like, Radha, "kick through" limitations placed on you by other people, cultures, or stereotypes?

In your WIT Kit journal, write about any situation in which you have not fulfilled your potential. What's holding you back? Are the obstacles external or internal? Make this the topic of your kitchen table group. Discuss this challenge and ask your friends for their advice on how you can climb the "mountains" on the path to your goals.

The WIT Kit
Exercises and Tools for Strengthening Your Courage Muscle

The bravest thing that you can do when you are not brave
is to profess courage and act accordingly.
—Corra May White Harris, writer (1869–1935)

1. In your WIT Kit journal, draw a vertical line down the center of the page to divide it into two columns. Label the column on the left "Imagined Fears" and the column on the right "Real Fears." Imagined Fears are intellectual or emotional fears that exist only in your head or heart. Real Fears are based on

something tangible—something that can be seen, that poses an actual risk to your safety or the safety of your loved ones.

2. Start listing everything you're afraid of in the appropriate columns. This can include anything from the fear of ending up alone to the fear that your preteen is having sex. They can be professional fears ("I'm not going to get that promotion I've been promised") or personal fears ("What's that suspicious-looking mole on my back?").

3. Go back and write down the worst thing that can happen and the best thing that can happen next to each scenario. Ask yourself if the worst thing that can happen has been exaggerated in your mind. What are the odds of that happening? What can you do to prevent it from happening? What steps can you take to reverse or resolve that situation?

4. Now, focus on the best thing that could happen. How can you foster a positive outcome? Who can help you? What three specific steps can you take to start acting on that fear instead of avoiding it?

5. Suggest to your kitchen table group that you have a conversation on courage. Share the fears and challenges you recorded in your WIT Kit journal. Ask your friends for their advice on how to overcome those fears. Ask them to share stories about their shining examples of courage. Make a commitment to "encourage" each other so you move forward on this journey together instead of having to tackle life's challenges on your own.

chapter four

Understanding Money and a Woman's Worth

26. When you are short on dollars, be rich in spirit.

I've been rich and I've been poor. Rich is better.
 — Greta Garbo, Swedish actress (1905–1990)

Self-Made Women
As one goes through life, one learns that if you don't paddle your own canoe, you don't move.
 — Katharine Hepburn, actress (1907–2003)

The four of us are "self-made" women. There were no silver spoons, trust funds, or college savings to launch us into adulthood. We were born into working-class families where living paycheck to paycheck was the norm. Collectively, the four of us have more than 200 years of life experience. Yet, when it comes to finances, we have made some embarrassing mistakes. Our financial DNA needed to be put on life support several times.

We carry a dirty, little secret that many women are guilty of but don't wish to confess: we believed that the men in our lives were smarter about money than we were. When that proved not to be true, we were left to pick up the pieces. That naïve assumption created chaos and crises in all of our lives.

Among the four of us, we have lost homes, jobs, and businesses. We have had to negotiate with the IRS on back taxes we didn't know our spouses owed (and didn't think we could be held accountable for). We've been involved in lawsuits in which we were implicated by virtue of our marriage licenses. We've seen our bank accounts drained nearly overnight and have been forced to trade in "champagne dreams for beer budgets."

In retrospect, our financial issues always seemed to coincide with our major life transitions. And, as with all transitions, we real-

SILLY RUMORS,
CHERYL — WE'RE
DOING FINE.

ized our financial crises could become a source of growth or remain a crippling failure. Their outcome depended on how we chose to react.

Women Hold the Purse Strings

"Your money or your life." We know what to do when a burglar makes this demand of us, but not when God does.

    —Mignon McLaughlin, journalist (1913–1983)

There is an irony in our personal stories that many women will recognize. Simply put, women have come a long way financially, yet we haven't come far at all. Women control 50 percent of the nation's wealth. Women have started 8 million businesses and created more than 1 million jobs in the past two decades. As a group, we earn more than $12 trillion every year. Women CEOs grace the covers of numerous magazines. Yet, somewhere along the journey, too many of us neglected to take responsibility for our financial health. In a world where more and more women hold the purse strings, the following still holds true:

- Women are first in America's growing hunger class.
- We live near the brink of poverty, when one considers that the difference between a mother on welfare and most other mothers is a partner's paycheck.
- We are unlikely to have a pension plan, yet we tend to live seven to nine years longer than the men in our lives.
- Fifty percent of us will become widows by the age of fifty-three, and 50 percent of us will divorce in our lifetimes.
- When we divorce, we are five times more likely to live in poverty after retirement than married women.
- For every year that we leave the workforce to care for a child or a parent, it will take us five years to make up the difference in our retirement and pension plans (United States Labor Department, 2004).

These facts are unacceptable. From experience and from the hundreds of interviews we've conducted, we believe most women will have serious financial setbacks in their lifetimes. Thankfully, there's something we can do about this. We can educate ourselves about money so we become smarter about the way we make it, manage it, and invest it.

The next three stories offer proof that you can turn around a bleak financial picture and a severe cash shortage. The ability to rise above financial ruin is within your grasp—if you learn from our mistakes and take action on some of the steps you're about to read about.

27. Learn the lessons from the dream house on Chateau Drive.

There are no hopeless situations. There are only people who have grown hopeless about them.

— *Clare Booth Luce, congresswoman and diplomat (1903–1987)*

If I Could Go Back to That One Moment in Time
Your whole life is a rehearsal for the moment you are in now.

— *Judith Malina, German-born actress (1926–)*

Jackie remembers their home on Chateau Drive. It was primarily financed as the result of the "three days on and three days off" shifts her husband worked as an emergency room physician. Little did she know their dream house would soon belong to someone else.

Someone who would never know about the Easter egg hunts elaborately planned and conducted in the backyard. Someone who would never transform the living room into a magical winter wonderland in December. To someone else, it would simply be a good investment. Yet to Jackie, the home was where her son had his own room, complete with a bright red bunk bed set his dad gave him on his fifth birthday. It was where her unborn child had been conceived.

"I remember so vividly our conversation regarding his life insurance. I kept nagging him to renew it. He told me he was too busy to take the required physical exam. He got tired of me bringing it up and yelled, 'Jackie! Are you planning to have me done away with? Is that why you are so persistent about this?'

"I dropped the subject. Three months later he was dead. I was left with an unborn child and a five-year-old. I had less than forty-five days to vacate our dream house on Chateau Drive—a house I could no longer afford.

"Today, I play back that conversation about life insurance in my mind. I wish I could return to that moment in time. I wish I had said, 'Steve, this situation is not about me. It is about our children and their quality of life if something happens to you. I am not being morbid. I am being financially responsible.'

"Since it's impossible to have this conversation with Steve, I have it with hundreds of women each year in the presentations I give. I beg these women, and I beg you, to stop being naïve. I implore them, and you, to have this tough conversation with your spouse, even if he doesn't want to talk about it. I explain that what happened to me could, God forbid, happen to you if you don't face your financial issues head on."

Are you on top of your financial situation? Are you and your spouse adequately covered by life and medical insurance? How much debt are you carrying? What type of savings or investments do you have to carry you over if you encounter tough times? If you can't answer these questions, you are tempting fate.

Promise yourself you will sit down this weekend with your spouse, or with a financial planner if you are on your own, and discuss all aspects of your financial health. Establish a plan so you can sleep at night knowing that you and your family will be provided for if your income is cut off.

28. Don't wait until your financial DNA has to be put on life support.

Money is always there, but the pockets change. It is not in the same pocket after a change, and that is all there is to say about money.
—Gertrude Stein, writer (1874–1946)

Simply Because We Are Women
Don't be afraid of the space between your dreams and reality.
—Belva Davis, journalist (1932 –)

Why do women take frequent financial tumbles? We interviewed several respected financial experts to help us understand why some women aren't faring as well as they should when it comes to money.

This complex issue becomes a little clearer when they told us that women, as a whole, still earn less money than men. The U.S. Labor Department documents that women working full time, year round, earn only 72 percent of what men earn. More than one-fourth of us head families with incomes of less than $20,000 per year. Ouch.

Women's work patterns also lead to less money. Due to pregnancy, child care, and caregiving, we spend an average of ten years away from work (versus one year for men). For every year we stay out of the workforce, it takes us five years to recover lost income, pension coverage, and career advancement. Over a lifetime, the inequality in our pay (76 cents versus $1.00) costs women $300,000.

Another piece of the puzzle is that women tend to live longer than men, which means we face a higher risk of chronic or disabling diseases that cut into our earning potential. We also routinely drain our bank accounts to pay the health care costs of a seriously ill husband, sick child, or ailing parent. Women pay a huge financial penalty for being the primary caregivers in the United States. According to a 1999 AARP/Brandeis University study, the loss of earned income due to women leaving the workforce to provide care is a staggering $678,664 over the woman's lifetime.

Several investment counselors also told us they believe many women still have math anxiety. It's a fact that seven out of ten girls' math grades begin a steep decline in middle school. Since many of us equate math with finances, the impact of this math anxiety on our ability to make and manage money is profound. Thankfully, it's also reversible.

Another reason some women are lagging behind in income potential is their mistaken belief that you can't be a "good person" if you're wealthy. One woman we talked with confessed she picked up that idea in childhood. "My parents were 'good people' who always taught us to 'do the right thing.' My dad was a teacher and my mom was a homemaker, which meant constant scrimping. My sister and I remember always ordering the cheapest thing on the menu the few times we ate out because we were so worried about our tight budget. When I went into the work world, a big salary was never my goal. I even remember saying that in interviews. When asked my salary demands, I would say, 'Money is not my priority. I care more about doing meaningful work that adds value.'"

Income Potential versus Income Reality

The person holding most women back from becoming high earners is themselves.

—Barbara Stanny, writer

"I was in my forties when I realized that making good money and doing meaningful work aren't mutually exclusive. A fellow entrepreneur told me that my 'service-oriented, altruistic' nature was causing me to undervalue my worth and undercharge for my services. She asked, 'Why are you so reluctant to raise your fees?' I answered, 'I guess I've always believed that old saying, "Money is the root of all evil."'

"She raised her eyebrows and corrected me with, 'You've got that saying wrong. It's actually "The love of money is the root of all evil."'

Yikes! This woman realized she had somehow equated wealth with misplaced priorities. She belatedly realized that you could be a millionaire and still be a quality person who is focused on making a difference in the world. She has since started valuing herself and charging what she's worth—she generates a healthy six-figure income while still being a good person.

'Fess up. Are finances just "not your thing"? Do you have lingering math anxiety that makes you feel you're not "good with numbers"? Have you sacrificed a good salary in order to be a stay-at-home mom? Do you not make as much money as you could because you're taking care of sick or elderly relatives? Did you grow up in humble surroundings and somehow acquire the mistaken belief that generating wealth is a shallow value?

It's time to assess your income potential versus your income reality. For now, what matters is not how much money you "could or should" be making. The question is, How much money are you making? Our purpose is not to discuss investment strategies. Our purpose is to persuade you and other women to take responsibility for your financial affairs, which means knowing exactly where you stand in terms of monthly revenue, outstanding bills, projected income, and available savings. The next story shares some specific tips on how you can get smart about making and managing money.

29. Realize that Ozzie and Harriett are long gone.

Women and girls have to own a part of the system—stocks, bonds, a business—if we aren't going to be owned by it.
    —*Joline Godfrey, business executive and writer*

Harriet Left the House without Her Cash
Ultimately, it is not the stories that determine our choices but the stories we continue to choose.
    —*Sylvia Boorstein, writer (1936–)*

The four of us were in New York, and we were excited! Michealene had set up a meeting with her friend, Gerry Laybourne. Gerry is the legend who created the Nickelodeon network, brought Big Bird and Sesame Street to TV land, and invented Nick at Nite. She wanted to talk with us about the book we were writing, because she thought we might have some good stories for her new Oxygen network, especially as it pertained to women and their finances.

We sat in Gerry's office and shared our financial ups and downs. Gerry listened intently. Then, she said, in the kindest way, that each of us was ultimately responsible for our financial state and that blaming our husbands for the mess we were in was unfair to them and less than brilliant on our part. We knew she was right. Although we were all educated, we were guilty of having "Ozzie and Harriet" mentalities when it came to money.

The 1950s television sitcom *Ozzie and Harriett* exemplified traditional male and female roles decades ago. Harriett was the classic homemaker. She always seemed to have an apron on, an iron in her hand, a loving smile on her face, and homemade chocolate chip cookies ready for the kids when they came home from school.

Today, Harriett would be juggling a full-time job with her homemaking responsibilities. She and Ozzie would both be commuting to work every day, swapping turns schlepping the kids to soccer, and divvying up chores on the weekend.

Yet one thing hasn't changed. Many women are still "delegating" their family finances to their husbands. Far too many women still naïvely believe that the men in their lives were somehow magically born with the "money management gene." Fathers, brothers, husbands, or business partners—women still trust the men in their lives with the finances more than they trust themselves. Ladies, it's time for us to grow up.

"*BAD TIME TO TALK MONEY?*"

The first step toward growing up and taking responsibility for our financial health is to educate ourselves. Do you read the financial section of the newspaper? No? It's time to start. Have you ever bought a copy of *Money* magazine? No? Throw an issue in your cart next time you go to the supermarket. Do you watch any of the investment shows on TV featuring investment experts? Yes? Good for you. No? Next time you're channel surfing and see Suze Orman, stop. Listen to her sage advice about the importance of clearing up that credit card debt. You might even want to buy her CD series. It's a painless way to educate yourself about money while taking your morning walk, jogging on the treadmill, or driving to work.

We've all heard the adage "Knowledge is power." We believe that acting on knowledge is what produces power. You don't have to re-create the finance wheel. There are plenty of experts who will save you trial-and-terror learning if you just read their articles, listen to their CDs, or watch their shows. But it's up to you to *act* on their wisdom so that money becomes a vital part of your life instead of something you think about only at the end of the month when it's time to pay bills.

30. Follow your cash so it doesn't end up in someone else's pocket.

Sometimes when you have everything, you can't really tell what matters.
——*Christina Onassis, wealthiest woman in the world (1950–1988)*

Women Have the Money Gene
One of the most powerful determinants of a woman's quality of life is her relationship with money. If she takes good care of her financial health, she lives life on her terms.
——*Cheryl Richardson, writer (1964–   )*

When women choose to focus on making more money and managing it wisely, they can create financial miracles. Several of our experts told us that all-women investor clubs consistently earn more than all-men investment clubs.

Why is that? Melinda Evans, a veteran Wall Street trader said, "Women have a lot of natural female skills that give them an advantage in the investment world. For example, they usually do more research and are less impulsive about their investments. Men tend to be less patient, which means they jump in and out of the market more often, which can nullify any significant gains."

The Inner Work of Wealth

Money will not purchase happiness for the woman who has no concept of what she wants. Money will not give her a code of values if she evaded the knowledge of what to value and will not provide the purpose if she's evaded the choice of what to seek.

—*Ayn Rand, Russian-born novelist and philosopher (1905–1982)*

Jane Williams is one of the experts we consulted. Jane had a vision more than twenty years ago to help women build stronger financial futures. She cofounded Sand Hill Advisors in Palo Alto, California. Jane chose to focus her practice on helping women in transition. Why? "Because it makes me feel good," Jane explained, "and because I believe a financially competent woman is a powerful person who can change the world."

Her company now manages $1.5 billion in assets, and Jane was named one of the "100 Most Influential Businesswomen in the Bay Area." In early 2005, she and Emile Goldman, chief wealth manager of Sand Hill Advisors, decided to form the Women's Wealth Network. Its mission is to "inspire, educate, and empower women to take charge of their financial lives."

Jane and Emile advise, coach, and cheer on women who are going through a transition such as a divorce, the death of a spouse, or a career change and help them plan and execute their financial rebirth. Emile told us, "Taking on your finances can be tackled in only four steps, and these steps can be taken regardless of background or current level of income."

Four steps? Everyone, no matter how busy, can handle four steps!

The Four Steps to Wealth
We must be willing to get rid of the life we've planned so as to have the life that is waiting for us.
——*Margaret Mead, anthropologist (1901–1978)*

1 Become Aware of Your Net Worth
Emile recommends that women begin by creating a net worth statement. Compile the total value of your assets and subtract your debt. The remainder is your net worth. After completing this simple subtraction problem, you are on your way to becoming a woman equipped to empower her financial future.

Emile recommends that women review their annual spending by going through their checkbook registry and credit card statements to develop a written picture of where cash is going. One may even want to enter the information into an electronic register, such as Quicken. Quicken is an easy-to-use and powerful tool that can help you stay updated on your spending and saving.

After you have a complete picture of your cash, begin to develop a budget and review it every six months. Gather up all life insurance, health insurance, and 401(k) and/or pension plan documents (which, if you are like many women, will be scattered in drawers throughout your house). Review these important documents and note anything you don't understand. If you couldn't explain why you're paying a certain amount

PENALTY SIGNALS FOR
FINANCIAL MISMANAGEMENT

ROUGHING
THE WALLET

IN OVER
YOUR HEAD

FAILURE
TO SAVE

FILING FOR
CHAPTER II
(BANKRUPTCY)

LOST SHIRT,
NO RESERVES

CHOKING ON
MONTHLY
PAYMENTS

BAD
RECORD
KEEPING

LACK OF
SMARTS

STINKY
INVESTMENT

for this coverage or what this policy means to someone else, then you need to ask a financial planner to explain it to you. Make copies of these documents and give them to a relative you can trust so they have a copy in case of emergency. Place the original documents in an accessible, fire-proof file box and plan to review them annually to keep them current.

Please note: Every year, people in Florida and along the Gulf Coast learn how important this is when they have to evacuate their homes quickly due to a fast-approaching hurricane. It's extremely frustrating and time-consuming to replace these documents if they're lost, and it can delay payment on your policies when you need them most—to rebuild or repair your home, for example.

The old saying is correct: Taxes, like death, are a certainty. Therefore, all women should understand their tax returns. Don't just sign them! If someone prepares the return for you, understand it is your right and responsibility to ask questions so you know exactly why you're claiming this, why you can't deduct that, and why you need to file a particular type of form. If, for some reason, the person preparing your taxes seems impatient or unable to answer your questions, find someone who understands that part of their job is to explain this process so you are comfortable with it.

2. Create a Vision

After you have calculated your net worth and created a budget, it is time to create a vision for your financial future. This is as important as getting a mammogram, but on the average, we spend more time picking out a new pair of shoes or trying to decide which DVD to rent on a Saturday night than we do planning our financial futures.

The financial vision you paint for yourself will become your touch point for making all kinds of decisions. Set specific money-related goals. Do you want to build your own a house, take a vacation to Europe, get your pilot's license, or create an emergency fund? Perhaps you want to buy a horse, start your own business, or set aside savings so you can retire at age sixty. Whatever it is, write it down and make sure it "lights your fire." If your plan doesn't inspire, you won't have the incentive or willpower to sacrifice short-term gratification for long-term financial gain.

3. Educate Yourself

You need to learn the language of finance. If you are intimidated or even bored by the subject, try to see finance in a new light.

Every discipline, from medicine to raising orchids, has its own language. Unfamiliar terms can make us feel dumb. Don't allow that discomfort or awkwardness to paralyze you. You don't have to be a day trader or broker to understand concepts like mutual funds, bull markets, and S-corporations. Take a class at your local community center or begin an adult education program. Visit a financial Web site and read the many free articles online. Seek out a mentor who is financially successful and ask her for her best lessons learned on how you can start creating wealth.

4. Engage Support

If you work for a company, have monthly allotments deducted from your pay and put directly into some type of 401(k) account that helps you save instead of spend. If you build that amount into your monthly budget, you won't miss it. Commit bonuses, certain commissions, raises, and tax refunds to a savings account or money market account. Consider joining one of the myriad women investment groups popping up all over the country. You don't even have to participate in person. Some conduct their monthly meetings by phone or via Web cast. Rid yourself of the common perception that you have to be "rich" to invest. It is simply not true. Remind yourself that starting small is better than not starting at all.

Remember the Two Truths

How many cares one loses when one decides not to be something but someone.

—*Coco Chanel, French fashion designer (1883–1971)*

Jan Yanehiro met Barbara Stanny, the daughter of the "R" in H&R Block last year. Barbara grew up believing her father would take care of her, which he did. She then thought she would marry and her husband would take care of her. She did marry, and had children, and she assumed her husband was managing her money, until she experienced an unexpected and defining moment at an ATM machine. She tried to withdraw some cash, and her account said, "Insufficient funds." How could that be? She should have had plenty of money in that account.

Imagine her shock upon discovering her husband had gambled away all her money! In what Barbara describes as a devastating but ultimately welcome wakeup call, she began a journey toward economic enlightenment. Barbara wrote a best-selling book entitled *Prince Charming Isn't Coming: How Women Get Smart about Their Money,* which we highly recommend. Barbara believes there are two fundamental truths regarding women and money.

1. Women don't need thousands of dollars to begin. Barbara has witnessed teachers, bookkeepers, stay-at-home moms, and others who didn't have a "big wad of cash" build a sizeable net worth using her techniques.

2. Women should not wait until a crisis to get started. Barbara says, "Too many women don't take responsibility for their finances until an emergency forces them into action. Don't wait for something to go wrong to get smart about money. All it takes is a decision on your part to 'deal with the big while it is still small.'"

We all wish we had met Barbara earlier in our lives. Her wise advice could have saved us a lot of heartache. It's not too late for you. We have included several steps in the next WIT Kit that can help you take charge of your finances—starting today. Please don't delay. These straightforward steps are doable, and they could make the difference between you and your loved ones living the lives you deserve or wondering how you're going to pay next month's rent.

The WIT Kit
Exercises and Tools for Understanding Money and a Woman's Worth

Prosperity is just around the corner for the woman who knows where to look.
—*Helen Hayes, actress (1900–1993)*

1. Schedule a half-day of your life to organize and update your finances. Instead of viewing this exercise with dread, pat yourself on the back and give yourself credit for taking responsibility for facing your financial facts. By taking the time to inform yourself about the reality of your net worth, you are putting naïveté behind you and acting like the adult you are.

2. Gather all your financial documents. That includes insurance policies; checking, savings, and investment account statements; mortgage papers, credit card bills, alimony receipts, and so on. Remember the equation "All That You Own Minus All That You Owe Equals Your Net Worth" and develop a clear statement of outstanding debts versus current and projected income.

3. Take out your WIT Kit journal and craft your financial vision. Make your words sing back to you on the page. Remember Emile Goodman's advice and create a financial vision so

compelling and personally meaningful that it motivates you to pass up tempting but less important purchases in order to save for your top priorities.

4. As part of your financial vision, write out your timeline and monetary plans for your retirement. What will you be doing? Where will you be living? How much will it cost? How are you setting aside sufficient funds (taking inflation into account) so you have enough money to take care of yourself in the later stages of life?

5. Call up a financially savvy friend and ask if you can buy her lunch or dinner. Take your WIT Kit journal and get her input on the practicality of your financial vision. Ask if she has recommendations about how you could better manage your money. Welcome her suggestions about how you could generate more income or invest more wisely.

6. Make finances the topic of an upcoming kitchen table group. Share your net worth with others and brainstorm how all of you could get smarter about money. Discuss beliefs regarding money that you might still be carrying around from childhood. Plan how you all can "grow up" and start valuing yourself enough to charge what you're worth and demand salaries commensurate with your talents.

chapter five

Learning to Live with Change

31. Never say never.

Many of our life crises are divinely scheduled to get us to change and head in a different direction.
　　—*Caroline Myss, medical intuitive and writer*

The Messy, Unpredictable, and Inescapable Nature of Change
All life is an attitude. There are a lot of people who feel sorry for themselves, and one thing I know for sure is that pity parties will kill you. If you do have one, dear, be sure to make it a short one.
　　—*Tammy Faye Bakker Messner, televangelist (1942–　)*

Have you taken those stress quizzes, the ones that ask you about the big changes in your life? The quiz allocates points to different sources of stress, including starting a new job, moving to a new town, and losing a loved one. The higher your total score, the higher your risk for a stress-related illness. When Jan took it, she tested off the charts!

"I was a widow who vowed never (ever!) to marry again," says Jan. "I was forty-seven when John died, so everyone asked me if I was going to get married again. 'Never!' was my constant reply, and I meant it. I met Rob on a blind date, and eight and a half months later, you guessed it, we were married. I will never say never again.

"Before Rob and I married, I put my home up for sale thinking it would take months to sell it. Much to my surprise, I got and accepted an offer before we even had our open house. It was a cash offer, with a contingency that I close and move in thirty days. I took the offer, packed up the furniture, and sent it to storage. I sent the dog to the grandparents, then took my three kids and the babysitter and moved into a hotel for two months.

"In less than three years, I had buried one husband, married another, sold a home, moved across two counties, enrolled my kids in three new schools, and become a stepmother to two teenagers, aged fifteen and sixteen. I inherited two dogs, one cat, and a dozen koi fish, and I started a new job. Change became my steadfast companion. I've learned that you have to look change square in the eye and embrace it with gusto!"

The four of us have come to know change as an irrevocable aspect of the human condition. For too long, we used every bit of our energy to maintain our status quo. Just when we thought we had experienced enough transitions for a lifetime, change would visit us again. We finally learned to surrender our Quixotic-like battle against change and embrace it instead of fight it.

We finally admitted to ourselves that, much as we wanted to, we couldn't control change. But we could learn to manage it. We could even learn to look forward to it.

Too many of us remain as passive bystanders, observing change taxiing down the runway at full throttle while we sit in the terminal

deciding whether to board. It's true that change, whether welcomed or forced, can be messy and unpredictable. It forces us to reexamine what we thought we knew, what we thought we could count on. Change dices, slices, and cuts to the core of our being. So how do we make change a welcome partner instead of a dreaded plague? We begin by developing a new attitude toward it.

Our Attitude Creates Our Reality during Change

What I like most about change is it is a synonym for hope.
    —*Linda Ellerbee, journalist (1944—   )*

Jan gave up searching for "whys" many years ago. "Whys" could include any of the following questions:

- Why did he die?
- Why did she drop out of the project?
- Why did I get breast cancer?
- Why didn't I save money?
- Why couldn't I have been satisfied with my old job?
- Why did he leave?

Jan says, "There are great mysteries in life that I will never completely understand, so I choose to focus on 'how.' I look for how everywhere. I ask, 'How can I make what happened work in our lives? How can we move forward? How can I help?' I still search for an occasional why every now and then. I don't think we can completely rid ourselves of the whys. Yet, I prefer the hows, because they empower me and give me a proactive attitude regarding change."

Our attitude is not something we are born with. That's good news, because it means we can shape it in ways that help us instead of hinder us. In fact, our attitude is the only element in our lives over which we have total control. In our experience, the most powerful way to shape our attitudes is to carefully choose our language when we talk to others and ourselves.

The words we choose and the questions we ask either support us or sabotage us. Words either fill us up with confidence or cause us to retreat in defeat. Throughout centuries, words have created wars and great love affairs. Words have facilitated world peace and helped overcome prejudice. Our words, whether spoken, written, or thought in private, have a direct effect on how we view the world and ourselves.

Turn "Woe Is Me" into Action
All that is necessary to break the spell of inertia and frustration is this: Act as if it were impossible to fail.
—Dorothea Brande, poet (1893–1948)

We can choose to describe a job loss as a professional crisis or an opportunity to move into a more rewarding career. We can describe a divorce as a personal failure or a needed wakeup call. We can conclude that a financial setback is permanent or purely temporary. The language we use paints word pictures that become our reality.

The four of us have learned to rely upon a series of questions to shape our "first response" to life-changing events. These questions help us stay focused on constructive responses instead of panicky reactions. The resulting language helps us concentrate on what we can do instead of what we can't.

What's the Good News in This Situation?
The question itself tells your mind (and your attitude) that there is a positive side just waiting to be uncovered. The question focuses mental energy on finding an optimistic instead of a pessimistic interpretation.

What Actions Could I Take That Would Benefit All Involved?
The question reminds you that while you may not control what's happened, you control how you respond to what's happened. It helps you concentrate on actions that serve you and others instead of going to the "dark side" and wallowing in how unfair or undeserved this situation may be.

Who (or What) Could Help Me Out in This Situation?
The question helps you remember that you are never alone. The world is filled with people who can help you resolve your issues if you'll just ask for their assistance.

We have found that if we approach transitions, whether voluntary or involuntary, with these beliefs—(1) there is good news, (2) we're in charge, and (3) help exists—it makes all the difference in whether we feel overwhelmed or encouraged. These three questions have helped us deal proactively with daunting circumstances that might have otherwise dragged us down.

Are you facing something daunting in your life right now? Take a few moments to answer those three questions in your WIT Kit journal. They can help you move from a "Woe is me" reaction to a "What can I do?" response.

32. Invent a secret language for change.

Life is a process of becoming, a combination of states we have to go through. Where people fail is that they wish to elect a state and remain in it. This is a kind of death.
—Anaïs Nin, French writer (1903–1977)

Creating Answers for the Dreaded Questions

All change, even the most longed for, has this melancholy. For what we leave behind us is a part of ourselves; we must die to one life before we can enter into another.

—Anatole France, French writer (1844–1924)

Seemingly innocent questions asked by colleagues during times of change can make us feel uncomfortable. After leaving a popular television show that she'd hosted for fifteen years, Jan dreaded running into people she knew, because their well-intended solicitous questions left her tongue-tied.

"Being on television for fifteen years meant my face was broadcast into the homes of hundreds of thousands of people. That was a wonderful gift, but it became a bit of a nightmare when I was no longer on the show. Almost everywhere I went, complete strangers would inevitably start the conversation with, 'So, Jan, what are you doing now?' I didn't want to go into a lengthy explanation, but there was no short answer to that question."

Jackie ended her term in the California legislature after a ten-year stint. "It was not my choice to leave, but by law, I was limited to the number of years I could serve. The timing of my departure could not have been worse. I was a new widow with a two-year old daughter and an eight-year-old son. As a public figure, I was often asked, 'What are your plans now?' It was a simple and appropriate question, yet I didn't know what to say. I would hem and haw and finally give a response I was never satisfied with."

One of the women we interviewed for this book, Nancy Olsen, said, "Near the end of my career with Imposters, I had been on the cover of several business magazines and was voted Entrepreneur of the Year by one of them. So, naturally, people would ask, 'What's next?' I was in the midst of recovering from a divorce, ending a business, and trying to figure that out. I was uncomfortable being asked that, because I didn't know the answer myself!"

"IF YOU ASK ME, THAT WOMAN WAS A LITTLE TOO HAPPY."

After a high-profile stint in corporate America, Michealene left to have children. "I opened up an office in my home and started my own company. I traded in my suits for blue jeans, and my work time was built around family time. I was always surprised to learn that few people thought I had a 'real job.' Countless times, I was asked the question, 'So now that you are not working, how do you spend your time?' It was if I had become invisible and powerless just because I had decided to become a different kind of 'working mom.' I wanted to scream when people asked me the question!"

Loss of Words Makes Us Feel Lost

Although the world is full of suffering, it is also full of the overcoming of it.
    —*Helen Keller, writer (1880–1968)*

When we are at a loss for words, we lose our power. We need to anticipate that when we're in the middle of a major change, the language we use will take on even greater importance. If we're feeling like a fish out of water, desperately trying to find our way back to the pond, it's in our best interests to anticipate the questions people will ask about our awkward circumstances. It's our responsibility to craft answers to those questions so that we can handle them with poise rather than panic.

We also need to deal with the emotions that arise when we discover that we aren't sure who we are anymore when the corporate titles, executive offices, and powerful acquaintances are suddenly gone. We may feel out of sorts and aimless. That's why it's important to consciously use words, when talking to others and ourselves, that make us feel in control rather than out of control.

The four of us acquired a secret language for these trying times. It was an acquisition made out of necessity. We didn't have the luxury of hiding out in our homes. Successfully navigating this transition required us to get out of the house and network with people who had the power to direct us toward new futures. We had to verbalize what we wanted and how we were going to get it instead of allowing ourselves to express our concerns. We have tried on many phrases and have test-driven them through some rocky terrain. They gave us an aura of self-assurance that we may not have had otherwise. Perhaps one or more of these phrases might help you answer your own sensitive questions graciously and confidently:

- I'm taking a sabbatical. I'm exploring some opportunities and interests I've neglected for too long.
- I've given myself a time-out to recharge my batteries. I'll probably take three or six months to do something different and then resume my business.
- Remember in science class, when you learned about the caterpillar and the process of metamorphosis? Well, I'm in the cocoon stage, on my way to becoming something new. I'm excited about the results!
- I'm in transition, taking time to choose my next path wisely.
- I'm so lucky! I'm being a kid again—learning, playing, exploring my options. I'll return to the adult world soon!

Are you in the middle of a transition and finding that people keep asking you well-meaning but embarrassing questions? Instead of allowing yourself to be tongue-tied, take the time to create and rehearse answers so you no longer have to dread running into people you know. Practice your answers in front of the mirror until you can say them with confidence.

If, for some reason, you can't come up with a satisfactory response, make this a topic for your next kitchen table group. Talk about the delicate questions you dread and brainstorm possible replies so you don't have to worry about your mind going blank when asked, "So what's new?"

33. Know that old habits hate being abandoned.

The only thing that makes life possible is permanent, intolerable uncertainty—not knowing what comes next.
—*Ursula K. Le Guin, writer (1929—)*

Why We Try to Maintain the Status Quo

Habits do not like being abandoned, and besides, they have the virtue of becoming tools.

— Anne Frank, German writer (1929–1945)

In reinventing ourselves, one problem we inevitably run into is our natural urge to protect the status quo—our habitual way of doing things. The good news is our knee-jerk resistance to change is a habit we can break. Perhaps the first step is to explode some of the myths we carry about the negative nature of change. We've listed four questions to get you started:

1. Do you talk about change more than you actually do it? Why? Unearth why you may avoid change—whether that's driving a different way to work, trying a different hairstyle, or confronting an in-law who's trying to run your life.

2. What is one thing you have implemented in your life in the past ninety days that demonstrates true change? Have you started going to the gym three days a week, no matter what? Have you started writing in your journal every morning, even if it's for five minutes?

3. Who is the most successful change agent you know? Why? What characteristics come to mind when you think of this person? Why do you think he or she embraces change instead of resisting it?

4. What would you need to do to cultivate the characteristics of the change agent you identified? How could you shake up your life so it's not same-old, same-old?

"HONEY, LET ME START BY SAYING THAT I, TOO, HAVE ANNOYING HABITS."

Saying the Unsayable

I began to have an idea of life, not as a slow shaping of achievement to fit my preconceived purposes, but as the gradual discovery and growth of a purpose which I did not know.

—Joanna Field, British psychologist (1900–1986)

We have found that one of the keys to welcoming change instead of running from it is to give ourselves permission to articulate what's going on in our gut, even when it isn't pretty or politically correct. This isn't just our discovery. Activist and author Gloria Steinem said, "Every woman needs an outlet for saying the unsayable."

Agreed. One of the reasons we came together as friends was because we all needed a safe place to say our "unsayables." We desperately needed a place we could say how we really felt without having to apologize for it or be embarrassed by it. In that forum, we were able to get out what we honestly thought but didn't dare say out loud. We were free to express such fragile feelings as

- I'm contemplating a divorce.
- I'm on the verge of bankruptcy.
- My husband is having an affair.
- I have a lump in my breast and I'm afraid it's cancer.
- My son is using drugs.
- I have lost my job.

An amazing thing happens when you are finally able to share the "ugly" truth about what's really happening in your world. Your friends offer sympathy and support so you don't have to shoulder that burden alone. You get it off your chest so you don't feel so weighed down and immobilized. Instead of it being a deep, dark secret you have to carry by yourself, it becomes something you see clearly and are empowered to face.

Questions Often Lead to Answers

Be patient toward all that is unsolved in your heart and try to love the questions themselves like locked rooms or books that are written in a foreign tongue. The point is to love everything. Live the questions now. Perhaps you will then gradually, without noticing it, live your way some distant day into the answers.

——Rainer Maria Rilke, German poet (1875–1926)

We've come up with a few more questions that bring out the unsayables so we can admit them and deal with them honestly:

- Do I live life in accordance with my standards? Yes? No? Why? What are those standards?
- Am I deeply satisfied with my life?
- How do I define success? Do I consider myself successful?
- What fills me up? What makes me feel like I am "enough" just the way I am? What keeps me from feeling like I'm "enough"?
- Am I living in the right place for me?
- Am I doing the right kind of work for me?
- Are my family relationships satisfying?
- Are my friendships satisfying?
- What level of "newness" do I need each week? What am I doing to bring that freshness into my life?

Make these questions the topic for your kitchen table group's meeting. Instead of going around the table and alternating answers to each question, give each participant twenty to thirty minutes to talk through her answers to these questions. Take advantage of this chance to fully explore your status quo to find out whether you're (1) satisfied with it or (2) yearning to make changes and just haven't had the clarity or courage to do things differently.

Agree up front to be completely honest. You can't improve anything if you don't first confess it is less than ideal. Once you have dared to tell the truth about your life, you can start planning how to make it better.

The WIT Kit
Exercises and Tools for Learning to Live with Change

Will you be the rock that redirects the course of the river?
—*Claire Nuer, psychologist, Holocaust survivor (1933–1999)*

1. In your WIT Kit journal, label a page "Changes I'd Like to Make." Start writing everything that comes to mind, whether it seems feasible or not. Remember, it doesn't have to make sense to anybody except you. Everything that occurs to you counts. If you think it, ink it.

2. Now, go back over that list and pick one "small" thing you can do this week and one "large" thing you can do by the end of the year.

3. Plan exactly how you're going to accomplish the "small" thing you want to achieve by the end of the week. If you want to get

back into morning walks with your friend, pick up the phone and call her right now to make a walk date for later this week.

4. Now, plan the first step to achieving your "large" change. What is one thing you can do this week to jump-start that change?

5. Next, plan a series of small steps you can take each week to make that large change a reality.

6. Ask your kitchen table group to help hold you accountable for making your small change and for stepping toward your large change, so you consciously and proactively make change a part of your life.

chapter six

Reinventing Yourself

34. Recognize that chocolate melts in order to take a new form.

I am not a has-been. I'm a will-be.
   —Lauren Bacall, actress (1924—   )

Everyone Has Meltdowns
Courage is not the towering oak that sees the storms come and go; it is the fragile blossom that opens in the snow.
   —Alice M. Swain, writer

Veteran news reporter Peter Fimrite stood squarely in the midst of death and destruction. Hurricane Katrina had left behind out-of-place items—a filthy teddy bear on top of a roof in Waveland, Mississippi, a Spider-Man lunchbox floating in the ruined city of New Orleans, displaced families on rooftops. These images told the tale better than any words could. And in the rubble, Peter expected to see many people crying. Yet, what he witnessed were survivors of Hurricane Katrina confronting their uncertain futures with a fierce determination to reinvent themselves.

"Everywhere I looked there was the search, not only for remnants of the past but for something inspiring that would serve as a vehicle for renewal," said Peter.

A woman in Waveland, Mississippi, was moved to tears, not by the sight of her destroyed home but by the discovery of her daughter's communion dress in the rubble. "That makes it all a little better," she said. Another woman, a grandmother, was collecting things out of the remnants of her destroyed Victorian home when she told Peter, "I'm in disbelief that we have to start over again, but we're glad we're alive. I'll let my family remember it like it was, and we'll regroup and go at it again." Even among the homeless and destitute left to fend for themselves after the Gulf Coast's worst hurricane on record, people focused on beginning again.

The entire world watched as Hurricane Katrina melted the lives of thousands and destroyed the city of New Orleans—a reminder to women that in all lives there will be days that appear totally devoid of hope. The four of us have learned to refer to these times as "meltdown days." These are the times when it seems our world has been turned upside down and inside out, when we do not know whom we can believe or what we can count on. On our meltdown days, we remember that chocolate too has to melt and that its entire substance has to change before it can be plied into a new form. It is a perfect metaphor to remind us that during the worst of times, when one has lost her entire "form," one can rebuild.

What to Do When You Don't Want to Get Out of Bed

If you've lost focus, just sit down and be still. Take the idea and rock it to and fro. Keep some of it and throw some away, and it will renew itself. You need do no more.

—*Clarissa Pinkola Estés, writer (1949–   )*

You awake on meltdown days wishing you didn't have to get out of bed. The world has become overwhelming. Events have stacked up to the point you're not sure you can handle them. You feel scared and immobilized.

What should you do? Give yourself permission to stay in bed for a day. Understand that your system is overloaded and needs a day to recuperate and recharge. Chances are, you have at least one or more sick days coming to you. This is what they're designed for. Take one now. Get caught up on sleep. Resist the urge to do paperwork, chores, or other "responsible" stuff. For one day, gather strength by nurturing and indulging yourself.

Make yourself a promise. Tomorrow you will rise, greet the day, put on your best face, and move forward. You will go back out into the world, determined to "fight the good fight" with renewed energy and commitment. That next day, after you have replenished yourself, call someone who cares about you and ask if you can buy that person lunch. During that lunch, talk honestly about what you're going through and ask for advice about possible next steps. Also, get in touch with at least one professional "fan"—a former boss or colleague who is familiar with your qualifications—and brainstorm ways to get back on track personally and professionally.

Getting Back "In Play"

Action indeed is the sole medium of expression.
    —*Jane Addams, writer and activist (1860–1935)*

An important part of helping yourself take new form is to "be in play" even if you do not know what game you are playing. "In play" means "out of the house." Being in play means being deliberately visible in your local community and professional industry so people see you in action. Only when people have a chance to spend time with or around you will they initiate on your behalf. ("You know what, you'd be perfect for this job!")

Once again, we're speaking from experience. Each time we made ourselves get up and out of the house, life got better. We gave ourselves one "personal" day to give in to the sadness or sense of being overwhelmed, and then we jumped back into life. And each time we forced ourselves back into play, something good happened as a result of that excursion.

BIFF'S FOR BURNOUTS

SOMETIMES KAREN NEEDED A JUMPSTART.

Are you in the middle of a meltdown? Has it been increasingly tempting to stay home with the shades drawn? Have you been avoiding friends and playing "hermit"? Do you wish you could crawl under your covers and make the world go away? This lack of action, called "checking out," is a form of denial. It is a slippery slope, because it become easier and easier to hide out. Isolating ourselves only makes things worse, because we end up spending all our time inside the emotional hell of whatever situation we are experiencing. We lose perspective and feel more and more helpless. We get locked in inertia.

If this is how you've been feeling, give yourself one day to stay home and recharge your batteries, and then resolve to put yourself back in play. Tell yourself you've had your quota of meltdown days and that it's time for you to assume your new form. Your new form requires you to get out of the house and reconnect with people who have the power to give you job leads, shore up your self-esteem, and suggest proactive next steps.

35. When dreams turn to dust, vacuum.

Hope is a thing with feathers.
That perches in the soul,
And sings the tune without the words,
And never stops at all.
    ——Emily Dickinson, poet (1830–1886)

Reclaiming Hope in a Field of Broken Dreams
I have found that life persists in the midst of destruction and, therefore, there must be a higher law than that of destruction.
    ——Indira Gandhi, former Prime Minister of India (1917–1984)

When dreams crumble, hope is the first thing lost, yet it is the most important thing we need to reclaim. Immediately, swiftly, and with a great sense of purpose, we must become hopeful and optimistic about our future. Jeri Becker is a wonderful example of someone who found hope hidden in a very bleak place.

Glancing at her credentials, one might think Jeri Becker moves in the company of the Bay Area's most dedicated social activists. She is a yoga teacher, newspaper and magazine writer, peer counselor, facilitator of a twelve-step program for women, literacy coach, choir director, and lay minister for hospitalized HIV and mentally disabled women.

Yet, Jeri Becker did all of her work behind bars at the Women's Correctional Facility in Corona, California. Jeri, serving a life sentence as an accomplice in a drug deal that resulted in a murder, has chosen to make the most of her circumstances. "I maintain my sense of hope, because to live without hope would be unbearable and intolerable. Without hope, I cannot live with purpose. But neither do I expect to live without suffering and adversity. There is an upside to suffering if we remain open to it. It draws us instantly closer to what really matters. In the throes of intense suffering, something which I call spirit arises from deep within me. And perhaps that has been the most important lesson of my experience. That the way out of trouble and pain of this life is in fact the way of hope."

Vacuuming Up the Pieces

Problems are messages.
　　—Shakti Gawain, writer

Isn't it interesting how Jeri found hope in the daily life of prison? Her story shows that no matter how dire the circumstances, we can have a fresh start if we take responsibility for bringing good things into our life.

Right now, you may not be able to find one "good thing" in your life. You may think, "Things are so bleak. I don't have anything to look forward to." Please trust us when we say that hope will help you open doors that now appear closed to you. In life-threatening situations, in times of crisis, when you are faced with the ugliest of circumstances, hope becomes a navigator that points you to a new place. It is the illuminator of paths and possibilities and places.

This isn't just our opinion. Dr. Jerome Groopman, Harvard medical professor and author of the book *The Anatomy of Hope,* says,

Hope does not arise from being told to think positively. Hope is the elevating feeling we experience when we see—in the mind's eye—a path to a better future. The path acknowledges the significant obstacles and deep pitfalls and has no room for delusion. Hope gives us the courage to confront our circumstances and the capacity to surmount them. We are just beginning to appreciate the power of hope and have not defined its limits. I see hope as the very heart of healing.

See? Having hope doesn't mean being a Pollyanna. It means consciously deciding to look ahead and figure out exactly how we can transcend these circumstances by embarking upon a proactive, pragmatic plan of action.

That is what we mean by hope. Each of us has had dark, dark days. And each of us chose not to continue to live that way. We're not saying it was easy to get up and get on with our lives. We are saying that choosing to believe that there were better days ahead, and then taking action to ensure that there were better days ahead, is an option that is available to all of us.

"WELL, DOCTOR, EXCEPT FOR SOME DEEP-SEATED CONCERNS ABOUT MY HUSBAND, KIDS, AGING PARENTS, FRIENDS, MONEY, WORK, RACISM, MORAL VALUES, POVERTY, CANCER, AIDS, SEX, WAR, CRIME, THE ENVIRONMENT, PANDEMICS, SHADY POLITICIANS, GREED, THE GENERAL LACK OF CIVILITY, AND MY ONGOING BATTLES WITH FACIAL HAIR, EVERYTHING'S COOL, I GUESS."

So, what are you going to do today to look ahead with hope? What is one step you're going to take to make tomorrow better than today? Who is one person you're going to reach out to? What is one specific thing you are going to do to build, as Groopman says, "a path to a better future"?

If you're not sure what that could be right now, our next story will be particularly timely for you. It explains how the simple act of choosing to be grateful is one of the single best things you can do to make each day a better day.

36. Be grateful the dog did not pee on the carpet.

Don't block the blessings.
——*Patti LaBelle, singer (1944—   )*

Gratitude as a Healing Force
Noble deeds, hot baths, and a count of your blessings are the best cures for depression.
——*"Dodie" Smith, British playwright (1896—1990)*

"Our days were packed with doctor appointments, medical procedures, and unending stress," says Deborah. "I was afraid that the stress was beginning to affect our two young children. Therefore, I searched for anything that would pull me out my sadness. A friend had given me a copy of a book called *Simple Abundance* by Sarah Ban Breathnach. One night, when I couldn't sleep, I opened the book and there it was staring back at me—the steps to creating a gratitude journal. I remember complaining to myself, 'What do I have to be grateful for? My husband is dying and my life is falling apart.' I did not have much respect for the concept of gratitude, but in desperation I decided to try it.

"My first few attempts at gratitude were not successful. Yet, each night, after everyone had gone to bed, I would sit in my favorite chair and write all that I had to be grateful for into a journal. My entries were pitiful! I wrote, 'I am grateful that the puppy did not pee on the carpet today! I am grateful that we did not make a visit to the emergency room tonight.'

"I kept this practice up for nearly two weeks, forcing myself to write down at least two things I was grateful for. My ability to recognize the good things in my life grew. Miraculously, I started feeling better. I cannot explain why it works. This is what I know.

"Cultivating gratitude in your daily life is magical. It affects your sense of well-being and makes you stronger. I remember waking up in the morning feeling rested and not sad. My husband's doctors even mentioned to me that they thought I had a remarkable spirit! I literally went from helpless to a serene and positive woman in a matter of weeks. My circumstances had not changed, but I had. Now, my gratitude journal is my first line of self-defense when events in my life become crazy. I have immense respect for its power."

The Science of Gratitude

You can judge your age by the amount of pain you feel when you come into contact with a new idea.
—*Pearl S. Buck, writer (1892–1973)*

The four of us resisted the positive influence of gratitude. You may also doubt its "healing" powers. When you're going through tough times, it can be hard to imagine that the simple act of feeling grateful can be such a life-changing tool.

Dr. Robert Emmons, professor of psychology at the University of California, has been conducting scientific research on gratitude and its importance for nearly twenty years. Funded by the National

Institute of Health, the results of his research match our own personal experiences with gratitude.

Dr. Emmons found that those who wrote in gratitude journals on a weekly basis also exercised more regularly, reported fewer physical symptoms, felt better about their lives, and were more optimistic than the control group that did not keep the journals. Participants who kept gratitude lists were more likely to have made progress toward important personal goals over a two-month period compared to those who did not. Dr. Emmons came to the conclusion that grateful people reported higher levels of positive emotions and lower levels of depression and stress.

NANCY CHANGED HER ATTITUDE JUST BEFORE WORK

In Japan, the concept of gratitude as a healing force has been studied for years. It is referred to as *naikan*. It means "inside looking" or "inside observation." Naikan is based upon two main questions: "What have I received from others that I can be thankful for?" and "What have I given to others?" In this Japanese tradition, it is believed that the greatest obstacles to gratitude are self-preoccupation and our sense of entitlement.

Self-preoccupation kills gratitude. When we are so preoccupied by our own thoughts, feelings, and needs, we have little attention left to notice what others are doing to support us. Neglecting the things that are truly working in our lives by focusing so intently on what is not working makes us less than optimistic.

The final obstacle, according to naikan belief, is the sense of entitlement. The more we think we have earned something or deserve it, the less likely we feel grateful for it. Our mistakes and limitations have a way of making us humble. They form a backdrop for future gratitude and a deep sense of appreciation for what is right in our lives.

Taking Stock

Appreciation can make a day, even change a life. Your willingness to put it into words is all that is necessary.
— *Margaret Cousins, Irish writer (1878–1954)*

When you are in the midst of a full-fledged crisis, identifying and cultivating gratitude may seem an impossibility. So how does one go about doing just that? Let's begin by taking stock in a very simple way. What are you most thankful for today? Perhaps a friend has the uncanny knack of calling right when you need someone to talk with. Perhaps you have a loyal pet that sensed your mood and came over and nestled in your lap. It may be that you can walk, breathe, smell, and see—and that you are thankful for your five senses. Whatever it is, you need to start identifying that for which you are grateful.

There is tremendous power, both psychologically and spiritually, in cultivating gratitude. The whole process changes your frame of reference and your state of mind. You can begin to compile a gratitude journal or you can simply begin like one of our friends does. She told us that if she wakes up and doesn't want to get out of bed, or if for some reason she's in a bad mood, she simply repeats a simple phrase, "If the only prayer you ever said was 'Thank you,' that would be enough." She told us, "I go from grumpy to grateful in seconds."

Are you skeptical? Why not try it? Tomorrow morning, if you wake up and don't feel like facing the day, simply lie in bed and count all the things you have to be grateful for. Repeat our friend's quote. Discover for yourself the power of choosing to focus on what's right with your world instead of what's wrong.

If there are quotes or inspiring passages from our book or another one you like, post them around your home and office where you will see them. Put them on your refrigerator, your bulletin board, next to your computer, in your wallet. When you are facing a challenge or simply need a mental pick-me-up, you can focus on them, remembering that gratitude is a powerful force. Keeping these ideas on how to live the best life possible "in sight, in mind" can lift your spirits and help you stay strong in the face of adversity.

37. Don't complain, create.

I was always looking outside myself for strength and confidence, but it comes from within. It is there all of the time.
    —*Anna Freud, Austrian psychotherapist and daughter of Sigmund Freud (1895–1982)*

Rising from the Ashes

The only thing that matters is the "stuff" that gets you from one moment to the next.

—*Mignon McLaughlin, journalist (1913–1983)*

Kathryn Tunstall was diagnosed with stage 2C breast cancer and given a 50 percent, five-year chance of survival. She underwent a lumpectomy and elected to do both chemotherapy and radiation. Eighteen months later, the cancer returned and she underwent a double mastectomy. At the time of her first diagnosis, Kathryn's two children were ages twelve and seven. As an executive of a medical device company, Kathryn began to use her knowledge of the medical industry to search for clinical trials that might improve her odds of survival.

"There must be a better method to link patients like me with potentially life-saving clinical trails," Kathryn thought. She began to search for people who could help her. Applying her business skills to the most important project she would ever undertake, Kathryn assembled a team to save her own life and also offer hope to other people with life-threatening illnesses. Literally from her hospital bed, Kathryn said, "I realized that there was an opportunity to meet the needs of patients and to provide better information to make better decisions." She launched Hopelink, a health care solutions company, and raised the first round funding to the tune of $3 million from the likes of Andy Bechtolsheim, cofounder of Sun Microsystems, and Ram Shriram, a former Netscape executive.

Many people join support groups when they face life-threatening illnesses. Kathryn started a company. As a result, Hopelink helped thousands of patients quickly find and enroll in FDA-sanctioned clinical trials. Kathryn Tunstall has beaten breast cancer. Alive and well today, well beyond the five-year mark, she epitomizes hope in action. She is also living proof that when things go wrong, we have the option to create something to resolve our problem instead of being content to complain about it.

When you least feel like moving is when you must move. Marta McGinnis Blodgett put herself into play as she sat in the cold waiting room of a hospital. Marta had carried with her some yarn and knitting needles to pass the time. She was shivering, and she thought that no woman should shiver and be alone while undergoing treatment for any cancer. As she knitted, she decided to knit a blanket that she could pass along to the next woman who followed in her path. Thus, "Knit for a Cure" was born. Marta and her friend teamed up with the largest wool manufacturer in America and inspired groups of women throughout the country to knit for a cause. The beautiful and warm hats, shawls, and blankets women knitted were donated to cancer treatment centers across the country.

Take the inspiring examples of Kathryn Tunstall and Marta McGinnis Blodgett as a reason to *go* and *do* something about your situation.

This is one of the most important lessons we've learned as Women in Transition. Many of the situations we had to deal with were involuntary. We didn't choose them, want them, or deserve them. In the long run, that didn't matter. What are you going to do to put yourself in play? How can you create, instead of complain about, this problem? Remember that steely resolve we talked about seeing in Jackie's eyes when she's determined not be victimized? What is one specific step you can take to resolve instead of run?

The WIT Kit
Exercises and Tools for Reinventing Yourself

I keep the telephone of my mind open to harmony, health, love, and abundance. Then whenever doubt, anxiety, or fear try to call me, they keep getting a busy signal and soon they will forget my number.
— *Edith Armstrong, writer*

1. In your WIT Kit journal, label a page "I Am Grateful for . . ." and start free-associating and writing down everything that comes to mind. If your mind stalls after a few things, look around the room and start noticing things you appreciate.

2. Each night, before you go to bed, write down three more things in your life you are grateful for. Even on bad days, force yourself to find at least three things. The very practice of *looking* for things for which to be grateful helps you develop a "grateful outlook," through which you start noticing the many things in your life that are going right. Furthermore, making these entries in your journal every night makes being grateful a habit. You are cultivating a mind-set of gratitude.

3. Begin writing a collection of letters to your children, spouse, and people who are important in your life. Tell them what you are going through, how you are feeling, what you have done to attempt to cope. Then, seal the letters. Don't send them yet. After you have successfully managed this transition, reread the letters. Write the ending to the story and share your lessons learned. At that point, decide if you wish to share your journey with the special people you wrote to.

4. Become an artist—yes, we mean you! Draw, paint, make over a room, plant a flower garden, do your best rendition of Georgia O'Keeffe. Lose yourself in expression and for the moment, forget your problems. The exercise will refresh you and make you stronger.

5. Make gratitude the topic of an upcoming kitchen table group. Make it a habit to start every meeting by going around the table and having each person say three things she's thankful for. When you make this a tradition, the group habit will support your individual habit.

chapter seven

Real Women Ask for Help!

38. Learn to laugh in the dark.

What saved me was my sense of humor and the fact that I had a good literary education.
    ——*Erica Jong, writer (1942–)*

Turning Headstones into Airline Miles
Facing a fate we cannot change, we are called upon to make the best of it by rising above ourselves and growing beyond ourselves.
    ——*Viktor Frankl, Austrian psychologist and writer,*
    Holocaust survivor (1905–1997)

Jackie's mind and body needed to rest. She found herself dreaming of going to Hawaii. That was the place where she always found a sense of physical and spiritual renewal. Such a trip would be impossible now: she was burying her husband tomorrow. Yet, the dream of fleeing to Hawaii with her young son and her unborn baby comforted her.

Almost out of the blue, a thought popped into her head. It was a tiny voice saying, "Jackie, you have to pay for the funeral expenses. Charge them to your United Airlines mileage credit card. After the baby is born, the three of you can take the free mileage and go to Hawaii." The thought at first seemed almost disrespectful. "Turn headstone charges into airline miles! What would the neighbors think?!"

That is exactly what Jackie did. She realized she couldn't bring her husband back, but she could take her children on a well-deserved vacation to a beautiful spot where they could reconnect in this trying time. She paid for funeral expenses (including the headstone), programs, flowers, and a burial plot with her mileage credit card.

Later on, Jan went through the same thought process and made a similar decision when faced with the left-behind expenses after her husband's death. "People don't realize that funerals cost a lot of money. I earned about 20,000 airline miles by charging all the funeral expenses. I always felt John would have been proud of me. He was a CPA, after all, and believed in using money wisely! I think he would have wanted me to take a trip with the kids after his death."

At first blush, the idea seems like the kind of dark humor only other widows would understand. Yet, we all have realized that dark humor is better than no humor. In fact, we have taught ourselves to laugh in the dark moments of our lives.

Remember earlier in the book when we talked about Norman Cousins's research into the healing power of humor? In our experience with traumatic transitions, we have discovered it's crucial to match the tears we shed with an equal number of laughs. We aim for the big belly laughs that make it hard to catch your breath. When you're going through dark times, it's natural to see dark humor everywhere, the kind that only another person who's been in that type of crisis can laugh at. Most of the time, this involves looking at life and its moments with a critical eye for the funny, the absurd, and the hilarious. Take for example, the following stories, short sound bites from our friends, family, and acquaintances:

Our friend had undergone a double mastectomy and reconstructive breast surgery. Through the pain and sheer terror of the experience, she said, "I have been flat-chested all of my life. I am not quite sure what to do with this new set of boobs. However, I will tell you that I'm looking forward to old age. These new boobs of mine will never sag, and I will be the hit, the real bombshell, in the senior citizen crowd!"

A husband, upon learning that his health insurance premium had been doubled because of his recent illness, despite the fact that his insurance company had promised they wouldn't increase the cost of his limitless, in-home oxygen supply, said to his wife, "Great! I'll open up an oxygen bar. They are a big hit in LA, and the revenue I generate should cover the cost of the premium increase!"

The group of friends that gathered at Jackie's house after the death of her husband was reflecting on the numerous people who had come forward to extend a helping hand. One friend said, "Jackie is a very lucky person to have so many friends." Another friend (Katy) responded with a huge belly laugh. She said, "*Lucky* isn't a word I'd use to describe Jackie. After all, she's been shot up and left for dead, and now she's three months pregnant and a widow! If that's luck, I don't want to be lucky."

Are you on the verge of taking yourself and your circumstances too seriously? Do you think it's disrespectful to enjoy yourself in the middle of a sad event? Could you turn this belief around and realize that dark humor is better than no humor? Could you realize that having a good belly laugh just might be the most therapeutic thing you could do for yourself?

Keep your eyes and ears open for the absurd in what's happening to you. Don't be afraid to laugh. It's not wrong; it's one of the healthiest things you can do.

39. Ask for help . . . and directions.

It's important to have a group of people whom you admire, can learn from, and can turn to, because it's just often too painful to learn it all yourself.
   —*Kay Koplovitz, cable television pioneer*

When to Ask for Help and How to Find It
My ancestors wandered in the wilderness for forty years, because even in biblical times, men would not stop to ask for directions.
   —*Bette Midler, comedian, actress, and singer (1945—   )*

"Looking back, I now realize all of the signs were there," said Deborah. "I needed help. Yet, I thought I was managing well. Somehow, I had convinced myself that if I managed my husband's illness like I had managed work projects in the past, everything would turn out okay. We had made six visits to the emergency room in six weeks. I was watching my husband for signs of respiratory distress, taking care of our two children, managing my own business, and cooking and cleaning. I looked like hell and had lost eighteen pounds.

"I GOOGLED 'ENTITLED TEEN' AND 'MENOPAUSAL MOM' AND IT DOESN'T LOOK PRETTY."

"The laundry alone should have been a clue—it was piled so high I could not get into the laundry room! My good friends would call me every other day just to check in. What I did not know was that they had secretly conspired to arrange for me to see a therapist who helped families face catastrophic illnesses. The day I entered the 'land of help' I thought I was going to lunch! My friends dropped me off at the therapist's office, and I had no choice but to enter. After all, they had paid for the visit and they were driving the car! Dr. Nancy McKusker offered me a lifeline that day. She helped me to develop reality-based solutions for my family and me."

As women, we are the first to give help and the last to ask for it. As mothers, daughters, wives, and business executives, we form the front line for caregiving. Yet, who cares for the caregiver? Numerous people can, but we have to let them know that we need it. Sounds simplistic, but knowing when and whom to ask for help and graciously receiving it are among the most difficult things a woman has to learn.

Signs and Symptoms That Signal Your Need for Help

I am treating you as my friend asking you to share my present minuses in the hope I can ask you to share my future pluses.
  —Katherine Mansfield, New Zealand–born writer (1888–1923)

Recognizing the first signs of distress can be difficult for women. We live in a culture where distress is often labeled "weakness," so we try to hide it from the world and sometimes from ourselves. We're reluctant to admit our human frailties. Unfortunately, this makes for a much more difficult journey than necessary. The following are some signs that it's time to say, "Help!"

- Your thinking isn't clear (and it's not related to hot flashes or a lack of protein in your diet).
- It is difficult for you to take action—the clothes you usually take to the cleaners are piled high in your closet, your son has no clean underwear, and your boss asks, "Is everything okay?"
- You are scared, and you just do not like the events and circumstances surrounding your life right now.

- Inside, you feel like an orphan in a strange land. Everything you took for granted is up for grabs. Instead of waking up to greet the day, you pray that you can just get through the day.
- You are either eating too much or you are forgetting to eat, and the stuff that you are eating is of the fast-food variety you swore you would never allow your children to have.
- People constantly say to you, "There is light at the end of the tunnel," and when they say it, you silently scream, "I didn't want to be in the tunnel in the first place, so how far away from the light am I, and how the hell do I get out of here?"
- You have received multiple copies of the book *When Bad Things Happen to Good People* from friends and coworkers.

40. Form a Merry Widows club.

I learned that I can't do anything about the length of my life, but I can do something about its width and its depth.
    —Letty Cottin Pogrebin, writer and co-founder of
      Ms. magazine (1939–   )

The Club No One Wishes to Join
Taking action is an antidote to despair.
    —Joan Baez, folk singer (1941–   )

There are times when women have to single-handedly invent their own help. Jackie and Jan did just that. Both had become widows with young children within a year of each other. As members of a group in society that no one ever wishes to join, they banded together to navigate the unknown challenges of single parenthood, death, financial tragedies, "dating," and work. They shared their fears and dreams. They helped each other cope with the loss of a spouse on a daily basis. Jackie and Jan call their bond "The Merry Widows Club."

"Our husband's gravesites are about thirty yards apart," said Jan. "Father's Day was always difficult to get through, so we decided to have a picnic at the gravesites to celebrate it. We brought Kentucky Fried Chicken, salad, and soft drinks, and my daughters, ages eleven and thirteen at the time, brought their boom box. Our boys, ages six and seven, brought a baseball and bat. Stephanie, age ten months, watched as the boys used the grave markers as bases—we didn't think our husbands would mind."

Since then, the Merry Widows Club has expanded in membership. Whenever Jackie and Jan learn that a woman in the Bay Area has suffered the loss of a spouse, they contact her and extend their hands of help. They help new widows maneuver through funeral arrangements. They orchestrate food brigades for months at a time so a new widow does not have to worry about cooking for a family. They have organized health teams, car pools, and finance teams to deal with the details that can be overwhelming to widows during their time of grief.

The Merry Widows gather every few months to talk, support, learn, cajole, advise, find out who is dating, and search for hope. Jan says, "They are such a comfort to me. Sometimes we speak about our lost spouses with laughter. Someone who hasn't gone through this experience wouldn't understand. At one lunch, we talked about what we put in the coffins. I put in a deck of cards and letters from the children and myself. Another woman put in her husband's cell phone. She actually called it! Another time we asked each other if our husbands would have remarried if we had died. Every widow answered with a resounding '*Yes!*' One widow said, 'The next month!' Now that some of us have remarried, we call ourselves the 'Merry and Married Widows' Club.'"

In the Merry and Married Widows' Club, we learn the lesson of commonality. If you are going through something alone, it's easy to think you're the only one this has ever happened to. That's a major benefit of support groups. When you talk with people who have experienced the same type of trauma, you discover that others have felt the same way and thought the same thoughts. Your isolation turns into connection.

Commonality is a minute away on your computer. Google whatever it is you're dealing with (the loss of a child, divorce, bankruptcy, getting fired) and you'll find Web sites with support groups and chat rooms where you can connect with others to share their lessons learned and draw encouragement.

41. Build your own "kitchen cabinet."

So life changes and you have to change too. I don't like change, but I've learned you just put your hands over your eyes and step off the edge.
  —*Linda Ronstadt, singer (1946–)*

Help Is a Gift—You're Worth It
We don't receive wisdom; we must discover it for ourselves after a journey that no one can take for us or spare us.
  —*Marcel Proust, French writer (1871–1922)*

One crisp winter morning, Jackie awoke determined to accept the help of those who had extended a hand to her after the death of her husband. It was a difficult decision to make, as she was accustomed to being the strong one at the table, the one who did the helping but not the receiving. She needed a sound plan for dealing with the very big issues her husband's death had created.

Methodically, she went through her list of people and found an accountant, a lawyer, a tax adviser, a real estate agent, and a banker. She invited them all to her home for a breakfast. Around her dining room table, this remarkable group of helpers assisted Jackie in devising a sound financial plan of action. This "kitchen cabinet" of friends left her home feeling gratified that they could contribute their expertise and their friendship to someone in need.

Help can come in the form of therapy. It also can come from those people in our lives who care about us. Help visits us in the form of total strangers who enter our lives in surprising ways. The first step is to be open to the fact that help is a gift we deserve. Accept it now. How do you let the gift-givers know you are open to help? You ask them. You also remember that the next time someone asks you the proverbial question, "Is there anything that I can do?" you are going to say "Yes" and make a request. To prepare you for your next encounter with a potential helper, complete a simple and short exercise in your WIT Kit journal:

1. Identify those people who have offered you help in the past two weeks.

2. What can they help you with? Make a list. (Hint: Tax advice, referrals to good lawyers, child care, someone to call when you are scared, steps to take, connections to those who can help, house cleaning, and so on.)

3. Think about why you cannot ask for help or why you resist it. List all your reasons. (Hint: Here's a list of some of the reasons we had for resisting offers of help.)

• I couldn't possibly ask for that. It would be a burden.

- I'm afraid. What if they say "No"? I cannot handle another rejection.
- I'll look like a fool.
- I'm supposed to be strong.
- I don't even know where to begin.
- People will think that I am crazy.

4. Review your reasons and let them go. You have much to gain and very little to lose. Pick up the phone, call the people who offered to help you, and ask them for what you need. You will feel better, and, believe it or not, they will too.

5. Now that you have asked for help, you may need some guidance in learning to receive it graciously. When someone steps forward and offers to help you, what do you do? Say "Yes." Simply accept it and offer a heartfelt "Thank you."

Promise yourself you will graciously give your helpers the gift of feeling needed. Tell them, "That would be wonderful. I accept, and please know how much I appreciate your thoughtfulness."

The WIT Kit
Exercises and Tools for Finding Help

Don't wait for something big to occur. Start where you are, with what you have, and that will always lead you into something greater.
—Mary Manin Morrissey, poet (1949–)

1. Do you have a support group? Are there people in your life who have gone through the same types of trials and

tribulations? Write in your WIT Kit journal how it feels to connect with people who understand what you're experiencing.

2. Identify two people with whom you have a lot in common. Reach out to these people and ask for their help. Talk to these trusted friends about your situation. They can provide an outsider's view and point out faulty thinking or misperceptions. They may even share a good laugh with you at what's happening and help you regain a sense of perspective.

3. Consider seeking a qualified therapist or life coach. Ask your friends or doctor for referrals, or check the Yellow Pages or online for a women's center in your area that has a list of reputable therapists.

4. Make "Help, I Need Someone" a topic for your kitchen table group. Ask each woman about her experience with getting help. Did she grow up thinking it was important to be independent and to "do it myself"? Does she turn down offers of assistance because she doesn't want to be perceived as weak? Create a new policy of graciously accepting help instead of rejecting it.

chapter eight

Facing Naysayers

42. Persist.

When you get into a tight place and everything goes against you, till it
seems as though you could not hang on a minute longer, never give up.
For that is just the place and time that the tide will turn.
  — *Harriet Beecher Stowe, activist and writer (1811–1896)*

Being a Different Drummer
Well-behaved women rarely make history.
  — *Anita Borg, computer scientist (1949–2003)*

The four of us have pursued dreams and lives that were out of the
ordinary for women of our backgrounds and cultures. Jan broke into
radio and television at a time when few women had on-air roles. She
started as a secretary and held on to her dream, and she ended up
with her own successful television program. Jackie wanted to be a
lawyer, and though she told everyone that she was "prelaw," deep inside she doubted that it would ever happen. Today, Jackie is not only a
lawyer but also one of California's most respected state senators.

Michealene always loved the movies. She carried around a dream
of becoming a filmmaker, but she didn't even own a camera! After
successful stints in corporate America, she traded in her suits for jeans
and hired someone to teach her how to write a script. She successfully
wrote, produced, and directed her first documentary. Deborah was
always intrigued by leaders—those who created paths and places from
small beginnings. Today, she works with leaders as a consultant and
writes about them in a variety of books and training seminars.

There are very few things in life of which we are certain. One
thing the four of us know for sure: smart women persist even when
success is elusive, failure has appeared, and the road ahead seems
unending.

In the remaining seven stories, we feature women who have overcome seemingly insurmountable obstacles and dispiriting individuals. They discovered that on the path to achieving dreams, you need to expect nonbelievers. These naysayers are sometimes innocent and sometimes intentional. Some do or say things to derail our dreams out of spite, while others actually claim to be doing or saying these things out of "love." We have all encountered individuals who tested our inner strength.

"YOU CAN'T LEAVE, LAURA —
I'M MADLY IN NEED WITH YOU."

Sometimes they were the very people about whom we cared most deeply. They have been our mothers or daughters, close friends or fathers, spouses or colleagues. These individuals told us what we could not do, be, say, think, or become. In most cases, they believed they had our best interests in their hearts. Usually there was some truth in what they said. We learned to harvest the truth and extract the value of what they said while staying devoted to our dreams.

Other people didn't have our best interests at heart. They simply wanted to thwart our dreams out of jealousy or . . . who knows what. Those types of people are called "energy vampires."

Energy Vampires Feed on Your Spirit

Thriving is what was meant for us on this earth.
Thriving, not just surviving, is our birthright as women.
   —*Clarissa Pinkola Estés, writer (1949–)*

Have you ever left a meeting or a social function feeling mentally or physically exhausted without knowing why? Judith Orloff, M.D. and clinical professor of psychiatry at UCLA, coined the term "energy vampires" in her book *Positive Energy*. Energy vampires are "takers." They lie in wait, ready to suck up every last bit of precious energy that you have. Dr. Orloff identified the different types of people lurking within your life and workplace, just waiting to suck the life right out of you.

Dr. Judith Orloff's *Favorite Energy Vampires*[*]

   We've all had them in our lives, but until now, we never knew what to call them other than difficult personalities! Both men and women are thoroughly capable of being energy vampires. Here are some descriptions of those sordid personalities just waiting to make the move on smart women in transition:

   The Sob Sister: She is always whining. She is the person with the "poor me" attitude. Offered solutions never seem to stop the complaining.

   The Drama Queen: She has flair, a real knack for taking everyday life and turning it into off-the-charts drama. To the drama queen, everything is a crisis.

   The Blamer: She has a sneaky way of making you feel guilty. She always has a negative comment to make about everything or everyone.

The Fixer Upper: She is desperate for you to fix her endless problems. Her neediness lures you in until he has monopolized your time.

The Go-for-the-Jugular Fiend: She cuts you down with sarcastic comments. Her vindictiveness spares no room for your feelings.

*Used with permission, Positive Energy by Judith Orloff, M.D. (Harmony Books, 2004).

During times of transition, we need to conserve all of our precious energy so we can be proactive rather than reactive. That means being on the alert for energy vampires who are trying to suck dry our enthusiasm, confidence, and vision. Review the list to see if any of these descriptions match someone at work or at home who seems to be at their best when you're at your worst. Next time they start to denigrate you, interrupt them and say, "If you have a suggestion on how I can succeed at this, it's welcome. If not, please realize that you are not helping me. Please keep your thoughts to yourself."

43. Listen to your beliefs, not your doubts.

I find that the very things that I get criticized for, which is usually being different and just doing my own thing and just being original, are the very things that make me successful.
  —— *Shania Twain, Grammy-winning singer (1965–)*

The World Belongs to Dreamers
We are volcanoes when we women offer our dreams and experiences as our truth. All maps change and there are new mountains.
  —— *Ursula K. Le Guin, writer (1929–)*

In looking back, Anne Robinson can understand how people thought she was marching to the beat of a very different drum. It was the height of the disco era, and John Travolta was center stage with *Saturday Night Fever*. Anne believed, in her heart, that people would buy good piano music, even in the face of naysayers.

Anne signed George Winston to her new record label, called Windham Hill. Her business objective was to create a company that sought to touch the souls as well as the hearts of music lovers worldwide. "I traveled up and down the California coast," Anne told us, "in a dilapidated Volkswagen Beetle selling tapes of wondrous music. I attempted to build a community of music lovers by getting to know them and to understand their interests.

"Today, we call what I was doing 'one-to-one' marketing! My sophisticated customer database was an old shoebox with the name, address, and comments of most every person who had purchased a Windham Hill record." Anne built her love for good music into a multinational company with a dream, a shoebox full of names, and an unrelenting passion.

REMEMBER — INTO EACH LIFE SOME PAINFULLY UNRELENTING TORRENTS OF HEART-WRENCHING RAIN CASCADING INTO CATASTROPHIC FLOODS MUST FALL.

RINSING SPIRIT-SAPPING CYNICS FROM MY LIFE, NO DOUBT.

Imagine a world without Anne Robinson, Stevie Wonder, the Beatles, or Barbra Streisand. A world with no iPod, electricity, or telephones. Just for a moment, close your eyes and imagine a world without the writings of Helen Keller, the courage of Amelia Earhart, the discoveries of Madame Curie, or the insights of Margaret Mead. If those individuals had listened to their naysayers, we would have missed out on all their talent, vision, and wisdom. Actress Jodie Foster said if she had listened to the naysayers of Hollywood, she would have never made a single movie. Debbi Fields founded a cookie empire by refusing to listen to those (including her husband) who thought selling cookies was a dumb idea! Naysayers have been present since Eve left the Garden of Eden. You've undoubtedly encountered some yourself. They say things like this:

- You need to be more realistic.
- Why can't you just be satisfied with what you have?
- You dreamer—always taking risks that never work out.
- Why can't you be more like (your brother, sister, friend)?
- If you don't watch out, this is going to backfire.
- Do you realize how much you have to lose if you do this?
- There you go again with your pie-in-the-sky ideas.
- You've always got your head in the clouds. What now?
- You're so selfish. You only think of what you want.

Since they show no chance of extinction, accept and expect that naysayers will be an ever-present part of your life's journey. That said, be very clear that you will stop listening to them. Vow to start listening to your dreams, not their doubts. Seek out people who tell you how you *can* make your dream work.

44. Take back your power.

If you think you're too small to have an impact, try going to bed with a mosquito.
    —Anita Roddick, British founder of the Body Shop (1942—)

Become Your Own Advocate
The most common way people give up their power is by thinking they don't have any.
    —Alice Walker, writer (1944—)

Michealene spent much of her early life waiting for someone to notice her talent. She hoped that someone would come to her aid and give her the guidance and/or support she wanted and felt she deserved. She was disappointed. "I can't say I magically woke from a deep sleep and valued myself one day," says Michealene. "After years of working hard and seeing the fruit of my labors go to other people, I realized I was the one who was giving away all of my power. I didn't have anyone to blame but myself. That was when I realized the only person who could rescue me was me."

Not all naysayers are external. All too often, the biggest naysayer in a woman's life is herself. Do any of the phrases below sound familiar?

- Oh, I can't make a living at this!
- This wouldn't be a real job!
- How could anyone find me attractive?
- I wouldn't be a good mom.
- How dare I think I can do this?
- Oh, I actually love doing this, but . . .

- Who am I to think that I could go after this?
- I don't deserve this.
- Oh, my God, what am I doing taking this risk?

Fortunately, we all have the ability to overcome the habit of being our own worst critic. Former American Psychological Association president Martin Seligman notes that many therapists are changing the nature of their work. Instead of delving into people's pasts and identifying what happened to them in childhood, many therapists are now concentrating their efforts on helping clients take responsibility *now* to make themselves more functional. He calls this "a sea change in psychology from focusing on what damages people toward trying to understand what makes them strong."

Do you have an inner judge who is quick to tell you how you are inadequate? Turn that critic into a coach. If that voice starts to tell you your dream is unrealistic and impossible, tell it the steps you're taking to make it possible. If this inner naysayer scoffs at your plans, remind it of Jodie Foster, Anne Robinson, and Debbi Fields. Then get up, get out, and make a difference in the world.

45. Refuse to be imprisoned by your past.

I know God will not give me anything I can't handle. I just wish that He didn't trust me so much.

— *Mother Teresa, Albanian-born Catholic nun and activist (1910–1997)*

From Drug-Addicted Prostitute to Georgetown-Educated Lawyer

Don't compromise yourself, honey. You are all that you've got.
    —*Janis Joplin, singer (1943–1970)*

Spend some time with Francine Ward and, immediately, you will be drawn in by her positive energy. She is brilliant, always impeccably dressed, and stylish. Yet, the Francine Ward of today is far from where she started.

As a young girl, Francine says, she got the message. She was told repeatedly that she would not amount to anything. She also learned that dreams were for girls who were rich, charmed, and white—not for girls like her. Francine took the message to heart and by the age of fourteen was strung out on heroin and well on her way to becoming an alcoholic. By eighteen, she was living as a homeless woman in the streets of New York. By twenty-one, she was supporting her drug and alcohol habits as a prostitute. At the age of twenty-six, while walking drunk on the streets in Las Vegas, Francine was hit by a car and severely injured. She was told that she would never walk again. This time, Francine forgot to listen to the message.

Refusing to be imprisoned by the challenging circumstances of her present *or* her past, not only did Francine learn to walk again, but she dramatically changed her life. "It was the end of my old life and the beginning of a life beyond my wildest imaginings," says Francine. Today, Francine walks through life as a Georgetown University-educated lawyer, the owner of a successful business, the author of two best-selling books, a loving wife, and a marathon runner.

Having traded the streets of New York for a home in the hills of Mill Valley, California, Francine attributes her transformation to something she calls "esteem-able acts."

"These are the conscious, consistent daily actions a woman can take toward becoming the person she barely dreams she can be," says Francine.

Francine is the kind of woman you can think about at 2 A.M. when you can't sleep because your life seems filled with insurmountable obstacles. She demonstrates that by taking responsibility for her choices and her actions, any woman can call forth the remarkable resilience of the human spirit. We're blessed to know Francine, and you can be too. Her book, *52 Weeks of Esteemable Acts: A Guide to Right Living,* is a treasure chest of wisdom. You can also go to her Web site at *www.esteemableacts.com* for more information—it's a good place to visit on a sleepless night when life seems at its darkest.

Resilience Is Something You Do

One's prime is elusive. You little girls, when you grow up, one must be on alert to recognize one's prime at whatever time of life It may occur.
———*Muriel Spark, British author of* The Prime of Miss Jean
     Brodie *(1918–2006)*

We four live in California. It is a place where people have been coming for a couple of hundred years to leave their pasts behind them and reinvent new futures. Amid the Hollywood movie stars, Silicon Valley success stories, and hopeful dreamers—after all, we live on fault lines!—California's pioneering state of mind has taught us much about reinvention and the power of resiliency. What Californians have known for years, scientists have just proven. Resiliency research conducted over the past decade has proven that all people have the capacity for overcoming odds and bouncing back.

Dr. Edith Grotberg of the University of Alabama, head of the International Resiliency Project, shared her research on why some people are able to bounce back and others aren't. Not surprisingly,

"SWEETIE, SOMETHING'S COME UP. MIND RAISING THE KIDS?"

her ideas on how we can overcome adversity echo many of the ideas we've shared in this book. Her findings include the following:

- There is no timeline, no set period, for finding the strength to overcome. Even one-third of poor, neglected, and abused children are capably building better lives by the time they are teenagers.
- Faith, be it in the future or in a higher power, is an essential ingredient in becoming resilient.
- Most resilient people don't go it alone. In fact, they don't even try. People who cope well with adversity are able to ask for help.
- Setting goals and planning for the future are strong factors in overcoming adversity and doubt. A belief in oneself and the ability to recognize one's strengths is important.

Dr. Grotberg said their most important finding is that resilience is "something you do, not something you have." In other words, it's not a characteristic you're either blessed with or not. It's a skill you can develop. It's an approach to life that you choose. Being resilient is a *verb* that is based on you acting on your own behalf. What is one thing you can *do* today so that you are not imprisoned by your situation?

The WIT Kit
Exercises and Tools for Facing Naysayers

Doing your own thing is a generous act. It creates obligation, which means you owe the world your best effort.
—*Barbara Sher, career counselor and writer*

1. In your WIT Kit journal, label the top of a page "Naysayers in My Life." Thinking back to your childhood and working your way to the present time, write down the names of people who seemed to be more interested in having you fail than succeed. And yes, this list could include you.

2. Go back over your list and write down anything you remember them saying or doing. Include the circumstances surrounding what happened and describe how their negative input affected you.

3. Now, close the book on those naysayers—literally. Put a big X across each of their names. Tell yourself you are going to take back your power and not let their attempts to undermine you continue. From now on, anytime you start to think of how

---

someone tried to derail your dreams, picture yourself X-ing them out.

4. Label another page in your journal, "My Supporters." List the names of all the people who have supported you, encouraged you, believed in you, said you could do it. Describe their positive impact on you and how support has affected you. Now, circle those names. Put big stars by these individuals. From now on, seek out and honor these supporters (and yes, this includes yourself).

5. Make energy vampires and supporters the topic of a kitchen table group meeting. Suggest that everyone do this exercise, and then give each participant fifteen minutes to share her insights. How is each of you going to honor the supporters in your life? What are you going to say the next time someone tries to derail your dream? How are you going to become more of a coach instead of a critic to yourself?

chapter nine

Rebuilding Dreams

46. Understand that success often comes disguised as a dumb idea.

No pessimist
Ever discovered the secret of the stars
Or sailed to an uncharted land or opened
A new doorway for the human spirit.
    — Helen Keller, writer (1880–1968)

Greatness Stems from the Dumb and the Weird

If you really want something, you can figure out how to make it happen.
    — Cher, actress and singer (1946–   )

In 1976, a husband informed his thirty-three-year-old housewife and their two children that he had decided to fulfill a lifelong ambition: to ride a horse from Brazil to New York. He figured he would be gone for six to twelve months. Imagine his wife's surprise!

The woman was Anita Roddick. Faced with the dilemma of how to support herself and her two children while her husband was absent, she turned to what she knew best. Concocting homemade cosmetics, lotions, and oils, she opened a tiny shop in the English resort town of Brighton, and the Body Shop was born. Today there are more than 1,000 Body Shops in forty-seven countries.

Kathleen Wentworth went to law school. She succeeded in her chosen path and was as a successful prosecuting attorney who aggressively put murderers, pedophiles, and other unsavory characters behind bars. Yet what Kathleen really wanted to do was fly. She signed up for flying lessons, and after getting certified, began to rack up the hundreds of hours needed in order to become a commercial pilot in any way that she could. Today, Kathleen Wentworth is known as Captain Wentworth. She became the first woman captain for United Airlines.

Nancy Olsen always loved jewelry, but she was never able to afford the real thing. With $2,000 borrowed from her schoolteacher's pension fund, she teamed up with artists and manufacturers to create replicas of world-class jewelry at prices all women could afford. Giving up the security of her teaching position, she opened her first store in San Francisco and called it Imposters Jewelry. In less than two years, Nancy had a thriving chain of nearly 500 stores across the country.

Laurel Burch had a passion for drawing cats—outrageously colorful cats. She painted them on everything—cups, scarves, earrings, and posters—and sold them on the streets of San Francisco. Today, Laurel Burch and her designs are an international brand, found in department stores throughout the world.

Condi Rice grew up in the segregated streets of Alabama where her father told her, "Even if you can't order a hamburger and be served at Woolworth's, that doesn't mean you can't grow up and become the president of the United States." Today, Condi serves as the first black woman secretary of state and is a close confidante and cabinet member to the president.

Rose Guilbault was the child of Hispanic migrant workers who made their living picking fruits and vegetables in the California fields. Rose became the first female in her family to attend college. She also became the first prominent Hispanic female television producer and host in the Bay Area. As Rose climbed the ranks in the television industry, she also became editorial director for a network television station in the Bay Area. Business executive and author of *Farm Worker's Daughter: Growing Up Mexican in America,* Rose held onto her dreams as a child and made them come true in adulthood.

Mimi Silbert took $1,000, a bunch of Christmas trees, and twenty ex-convicts to begin an experiment that grew into Delancey Street—one of the most successful rehabilitation programs in the world. Running for-profit operations staffed by ex-convicts and former drug addicts, Mimi and her staff are the successful owners of a restaurant, a bookstore, a construction company, a moving company, and, yes, still the best damn Christmas tree lot in San Francisco.

Kristi Yamaguchi was born with deformed feet. Her tiny feet pointed inward and curled under. For the first two years of her life, she wore plaster casts and foot braces. As therapy for her feet, her parents enrolled her in dance, ballet, and tap lessons. Yet it was ice skating that captured her heart. As a youngster, she would wake daily at 4 A.M. to practice on the ice for five hours before heading to school. Ironically, when she was selected to represent the United States at the 1992 Olympics, she was considered the underdog. Yet Kristi's dream came true when she won the gold medal at the Winter Olympics, in Albertville, France, that year.

When these women were devising their dreams, they were often told that their plans were "dumb." We've come to understand that success often comes disguised as a "dumb" idea—at least to others. We prefer ex-Beatle Paul McCartney's interpretation. "It's not the people who are doing 'weird' things that are weird. It's the people who are calling people weird who are weird!" Bravo. We agree that pioneers and dreams may be called "dumb and weird," but their inventions and creations have changed the world for the better.

Could your idea just be ahead of its time? Are people telling you it's crazy just because it's not already common? Maybe you are a pioneer who is daring to be the first at something instead of blending in with the pack. Could you seek out fellow inventors or creative types who will support your innovation instead of sabotage it?

47. Seek a dream catcher.

Dreams are illustrations from the book your soul is writing about you.
    —*Marsha Norman, playwright (1947–   )*

The Power of Dreaming
Rose-colored glasses are never made in bifocals. Nobody wants to read the small print in dreams.
    —*Ann Landers, advice columnist (1918–2002)*

Ola Kizer wanted a college degree, and at the age of eighty-six, she finally got it by becoming the oldest undergraduate in more than 200 years at the University of Tennessee. Vowing to never again return to the poverty she knew as a child, she figured the college degree would help her. "You have to hold onto your dreams," Kizer said. "It is not going to be easy. If you are rowing, you couldn't cross the ocean in one day. So stick with it and keep going." Ola Kizer knows the power behind dreaming.

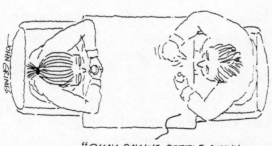

"OKAY, SAY WE SETTLE DOWN
AND HAVE A NICE LIFE TOGETHER.
WHAT'S IN IT FOR ME?"

Your dreams may not be as large and encompassing as Indira Gandhi's was in saving her native country of India or as courageous as Amelia Earhart's when she took to the skies. You may or may not set your sights on inventing the next best-selling product or book, but your dream and your visions for your life are just as important. In fact, they are vitally important to your health and well-being.

How does one begin? We posed that question to America's Dream Coach, Marcia Wieder. Jackie Speier first met Marcia twenty-five years ago. This was before Marcia's two best-selling books, before her numerous appearances on the *Today Show* and *Oprah*. Way before Marcia's own PBS television special. Jackie met Marcia when she was just beginning to dream.

Today, Marcia Wieder has spent nearly two decades helping women and men achieve their dreams. Just as writers focus on the structure of a paragraph and the elements needed to form a complete thought, Marcia suggests that women should focus on the four Ps: purpose, passion, possibilities, and power. The four Ps can help you become the author of your own life. Perhaps most important, Marcia reminds us it is never too late to redesign your purpose, no matter your age or situation. She says, "Power is derived from acting on your dreams and measuring your results against your own internal scale of excellence."

Rules for Dreamers

Great dreams . . . never even get out of the box. It takes an uncommon amount of guts to put your dreams on the line, to hold them up and say, "How good or how bad am I?" That's where courage comes in.
— *Erma Bombeck, humorist and writer (1927–1996)*

Many years ago, Deborah learned of a "dream catcher." His name is Dr. Ivan Scheier. During his long career, Dr. Scheier helped hundreds of nonprofit organizations and communities achieve their dreams. As

a consultant to presidents and mayors, Scheier spent his life developing citizen volunteers to better improve America's communities. At
the age of seventy-eight, Dr. Scheier created VOLUNTAS, a resi-
dence retreat aimed at stimulating creative, expansive, and practical
dreaming about communities and volunteerism.

"A world in which people have no chance of achieving their dreams
is not, to me, a world in which I would choose to live," says Scheier. In
his role as dream catcher, Dr. Scheier listened to hundreds of people
with ideas, hopes, and inspirations who lacked the financial resources
to bring their dreams to life. He developed some rules for dreamers
that smart women can use in making their dreams come true:

1. Realize that nothing happens right away. Stay with your dream
   and live close to your beliefs.

2. Dreams usually don't come about in the way that you first visualize them, so don't expect them to. Be open to new opportunities and ideas. Reality is too complicated, and surprise is half
   the fun!

3. The only constants are your values. Keep compromise to a
   minimum on these even when they come disguised in nice
   names like team building, negotiation, or consensus.

4. Seek cooperators in your dream. Dreams rarely survive their
   origins without evolution to a broader ownership. Get your
   ideas out in the universe and see who they inspire.

5. Be as flexible about implementation of your dream as you are
   uncompromising on the values of your vision. Avoid tight
   planning, and don't let your plan become an end in itself.

6. Money is never the main ingredient of dream achievement. Free yourself from major money needs insofar as it is reasonable and possible. The "if only I had the money" mind-set can result in neglect of other potentially more feasible approaches.

7. When you get the blues—and dreamers do—don't look forward; look backward. Looking backward reminds you how many dreams have actually come true in your life, while looking forward only reminds you of the obstacles you face.

Please review these seven suggestions. Pick one that is particularly timely or relevant for you and discuss it at your kitchen table group. Perhaps it is number seven—the counterintuitive idea to look backward instead of forward. Reviewing your history and tapping into your successes could be just what you need to help you forge ahead with determination.

48. Schedule a paint date.

Never mistake knowledge for wisdom. One helps you make a living; the other helps you make a life.
   —*Eleanor Roosevelt, former first lady (1884–1962)*

Painting with the Presbyterian Women
Life is what we make it—always has been and always will be.
   —*Grandma Moses, painter (1860–1961)*

"Every other Saturday morning began my introduction to the wisdom of women and its importance in rebuilding dreams," says Deborah. "The journey began with a woman in my neighborhood who had learned of my husband's illness. She wanted me to paint with her. She insisted that I was an artist, even though I told her that my best attempt in art was a project in fifth grade consisting of glue, some crayons, and Popsicle sticks all thrown together. She continued to badger me until I agreed to visit her garage and paint, if only to get her to quit pestering me!

"The 'paint date' rolled around, and I reluctantly appeared at her garage. Her two-car garage had been transformed into a wonderfully decorated and inviting art studio. I was not the only invited guest that day. The studio was overflowing with women, ranging in age from twenty-five to eighty-six. They were members of the local Presbyterian women's group.

"Over coffee, tea, and fresh fruit, in the garage, we painted on canvas and talked for nearly three hours. In those three hours, the women brought more collective wisdom into my life than I had encountered in three years. The older women in the group were mirrors for the young. Their life experiences resulted in valuable advice and wisdom that was uplifting and encouraging. The younger women adored the elders and provided a source of connection to the community that they cherished.

"My introduction in the garage morphed into an every-other-Saturday excursion with the Presbyterian women's group. Although I am neither a Presbyterian nor an artist, it didn't seem to matter to them. What mattered was that I was a woman in their community who needed to be supported through a transition.

"These gatherings filled me up with a special form of women's wisdom that always made me yearn for more. I shared stories about this soul-satisfying experience with other women. That's when I realized that many women wanted to find and interact with women of wisdom."

I Needed to Find "Me"

Of any stopping place in life, it is good to ask whether it will be a good place from which to go on as well as a good place to remain.
——*Mary Catherine Bateson, anthropologist (1939—   )*

Jan had a similar experience. Instead of painting, she went to breakfast—a breakfast that would give birth to a whole new outlook on life. "I was feeling low," said Jan. "Depressed might be another word for it. I no longer had the best television job in the world, and my husband had recently died. I was putting on lipstick in the morning, kissing my kids, dealing with lawsuits, and I felt completely lost. I needed a job; I needed to support my kids. Truthfully, what I needed was to find 'me.'

"One of my best friends, Debbi Fields (founder of Mrs. Fields Cookies) was coming to visit. I used her as the perfect excuse to gather some incredible women for a breakfast I knew would be uplifting. Gathered round that morning were Debbi Fields, Jackie Speier, Nancy Olsen, Linda Howell, Anne Robinson, and Susie Tompkins. We shared fears, concerns, self-doubt, and lots of laughter.

"Debbi told us what it is like to be newly divorced after twenty years of marriage and five children. (Today, Debbi is remarried and has added five stepchildren to her family!) Jackie spoke of learning to date after the death of her husband and running for the State Senate. (Today, she is married and is a state senator!)

"Nancy talked of growing her company from one store to 126 nationwide, bringing in venture capital money and subsequently being fired with no severance, no golden parachute, nothing. (Today, Nancy is a high school counselor, having retuned to her first love of teaching. She also plays percussion in a local concert band!)

"Linda told us how she gave up her marketing career for her family and wondered aloud about her value. (Today, she has no doubt about her decision.) Anne told us that this was the first day she was 'unemployed.' She had sold her company, and the new owners were exercising their option to remove her from the helm four years earlier than originally agreed. (Anne has since formed a textile company and a music company, and she swims every day.) Susie told us how she had survived the public disintegration of her marriage and the story behind her company, Esprit. (Today, Susie is married to her high school sweetheart, Mark Buell, and they are living happily ever after!)

"I remember feeling such an enormous amount of respect for each of these women. I also remember how good I felt—how empowered. It was a feeling that lasted for a long time afterward. The gathering for breakfast helped me realize I was not alone. We were all women in transition. A few days later, Jackie decided that our breakfast conversation should go on. She wanted us to join her at the Professional and Business Women's Conference and thought our 'breakfast topic' would be a great seminar. This was the beginning of our kitchen table group of friends. We called ourselves WIT— Women in Transition—and our conversations continue today."

What Is Wisdom?

Look at everything as though you were seeing it either for the first or last time.

    —*Betty Smith, writer (1896–1972)*

If you ever feel as though your shoulders are scraping the cement sidewalk, remember what Deborah found in the garage and what Jan discovered over breakfast: women have a remarkable way of helping other women. The wisdom of women can be a life raft when you are in the midst of a transition. When you get together with them, they always tell you how fabulous you are even when you don't feel fabulous!

Wisdom is not something we are born with. It is a cumulative result of life lessons gained through personal experience. The good news is we can "borrow" wisdom from other people so we can learn from their experiences without having to experience everything ourselves.

By accessing people who have "been there, done that," we can capitalize on their successes and avoid their errors. The best news is that collective wisdom is available to every woman, no matter her community, background, or education. All she has to do is reach out to those around her who are willing to share their insights and observations, and who have some of the characteristics that Abraham Maslow identified as being "wise."

Famed psychologist Abraham Maslow saw wisdom as an important criterion in his landmark study of self-actualization. From Maslow, we learn that wise people see things clearly. They act in prudent and effective ways and possess a deep understanding of the human condition. Wise people are able to handle whatever arises in their lives with peace of mind and with effective and compassionate responses. They are in control of important emotions such as fear, anger, jealousy, hatred, and greed, for they know such emotions are the cause of human suffering.

Wise people have strong ethical boundaries and use intuition and intellect to resolve conflicts. According to Maslow, wise people live compassionately. They take full responsibility for their choices and actions and maintain a positive outlook on life, no matter the circumstances.

How Does One Find Wisdom?

To know the road ahead, ask those coming back.
— *Chinese proverb*

We've come to believe that we need at least three wise women in our lives. These mentors share how they have faced and overcome difficulties, and how we can do the same. By "going before us," they have learned what works and what doesn't. We no longer have to re-create the wheel, because we have the benefit of their experiences and support.

You may be thinking, "I agree, but where do I find one wise woman, much less three?" Trust us when we say that wise women are everywhere. They can be found among our family members, in our workplaces, in organizations and churches, and certainly in every community around the world. All she has to do is reach out to those around her who are willing to share their insights and observations.

Start by looking around and asking yourself, "Whom do I admire? Who is someone I respect for what she has accomplished or overcome? Who is someone who has been down the path I'm about to start?"

You may be thinking, "This person is busy. Why would she want to help me?" Good question. She'll want to help you if you honor the Three As of being a protégé. When you approach her, make sure your first words are, "I know you are busy, but may I have five minutes of your time?" This is a gracious way to let the woman know you're considerate of her other demands.

Next *ask*, "I'm _____ (about to have my first child/interested in launching my own business). Would you be willing to share a couple of things you wish someone had told you when you were starting out?" Take notes so the wise woman realizes how much you honor her input.

Be sure to thank her at that moment and tell her how you intend to *act* on her suggestions. Then get back in touch to let her know how her advice worked out and how much you *appreciate* her contribution. If you *ask, act,* and *appreciate,* you have made this a win-win situation for you and for the woman who has generously shared her wisdom.

49. Find three wise women.

Without self-confidence and wisdom, we are as babes in the cradle. And how can we generate this imponderable quality, which is yet so invaluable, most quickly?
    —— *Virginia Woolf, British writer (1882–1941)*

The Wise Women Tour
If you ask me what I came into this world to do, I will tell you: I came to live my life out loud.
    —— *Emile Zola, French novelist and critic (1840–1902)*

We are so convinced that every woman needs at least three wise women, we think there should be a Wise Woman Council, complete with a toll-free 800 number where women could call to talk to a wise woman any time of the day. Since this council does not yet exist, we decided to prove that in every community around the world, wise women were residing, simply waiting to be discovered. So we launched the Wise Woman Tour™ to prove how easily one can connect with women of wisdom. We did this by word of mouth—telling everyone we knew about our search. We sent out e-mails. We researched. When a story appeared in the local papers about a woman, we picked up the phone and called her. Word spread quickly about our search. As a result, we were introduced to some remarkable women.

Trading Manhattan for a Petrified Forest
You must first be who you really are, then do what you need to do in order to have what you want.
    —— *Margaret Young, singer (1900–1969)*

The four of us—Jan, Jackie, Michealene, and Deborah—were sitting at a cloth-covered table surrounded by photographs of Nobel Prize winners and presidents in the Stanford University faculty club. We were waiting for Sarah Little Turnbull, often referred to as America's "mother of invention." Into the faculty club walked a small wisp of a woman with an infectious smile. Wearing a black beret, a strand of pearls, and a large upside-down clock that sat right in the middle of her black sweater, Sarah introduced herself. We learned that she had just returned from a vacation in Hawaii in celebration of her eighty-second birthday.

Naturally, our first question for Sara was the story behind the upside-down clock. Sarah said the timepiece represented efficiency in her life, sleek design, compassion, and time for others. They were, she said, the very values that mattered most to her.

Sarah is a leading consultant to major corporations all over the world. Working with companies such as Coca-Cola, 3M, and Proctor & Gamble, the chairman of Revlon once said that Sarah was his secret weapon. However, the contribution she is most famous for is the development of CorningWare.

In the 1950s the Corning Company needed a new use for Pyroceram, a material used for missiles that could withstand intense heat and freezing cold. Realizing that women would remain in the workforce after the war and still be responsible for household duties, Sarah turned Pyroceram into CorningWare! The day we met with Sarah, she was heading up the Change Process Laboratory in the Stanford Graduate School of Business, a position she still holds today at the age of eighty-eight.

One remarkable chapter in Sarah Little Turnbull's life began with love. In 1965, Sarah met Jim Turnbull and married him, leaving behind the high-powered New York executive life she had known. Sarah traded her car, driver, penthouse, and Manhattan for a life with Jim in the Gingko Petrified Forest, along the Columbia River in Washington State. Replacing New York City for a town with just forty-five people, not to mention the high-society life, must have been a difficult transition. Surprisingly, Sarah told us, "I missed none of it. Other values took the place of those things. Being in love was the turning point."

From the Petrified Forest, Sarah continued her trailblazing in corporate America. In 1988, she brought her ailing husband to the Stanford Medical Center in search of medical expertise for the brain cancer he was suffering from. She fell in love with the area and promptly moved to California. Sarah's husband died in 1991, and although his loss is still with her, she has cultivated a large family of friends, former students, and staff.

Sarah Little Turnbull's wisdom is the stuff of legend. "I just happen to value the phenomenon of life and the opportunity to serve in society. That is what keeps me going. I need to keep involved, to be part of the music of life. It's more than enough to get you going each morning. My doctor once told me that I had to realize that I'm a frail little old lady, and I said, 'Well, that had never occurred to me!' I don't think the numbers matter at all. It's what you're doing with your minutes. I'm constantly stirring the pot. It's what I am about, and it is what I think youth is."

Finding Wisdom around the World
If you have knowledge, let others light their candles in it.
—Margaret Fuller, writer (1810–1850)

Our search took us from the Stanford faculty club to the town of imaginary heroes and movie stars. Hollywood is home to Margaret Loesch, a four-time Emmy winner who built the Fox Kids Network from a start-up to the number one children's television service in the country. Prior to her tenure with Fox, Margaret was president and chief executive officer of Marvel Productions and Hanna-Barbera Productions, where she supervised the development of more than thirty television series. Michealene was referred to Margaret through her former boss. Michealene said, "I always respected and admired who she was. The one thing about Margaret that always stood out was her integrity."

When asked about this, Margaret said, "The truer you are to yourself, the less conflicted you will be in life. In my experience, women are loyal and competent and often optimistic. Many people appreciate integrity, honesty, and dependability, but unfortunately, it's not necessarily what is rewarded in business. Every major mistake in my life has come from my making an assumption. The most career-impacting assumption I've made has been to believe that I would be taken care of. Never make assumptions. Today when I speak to women, I pass on this hard-learned wisdom. Negotiate your exit package before you start anything—a job, a marriage, a partnership. Don't assume that someone else will be there to take care of your interests."

The next stop on the wise women tour took us to New York to speak with Gerry Laybourne. Gerry's two passions in life revolve around women and children. You may know Gerry from her reputation and stellar success in Hollywood, which includes experience at Lifetime Television and ABC/Disney, and starting and operating Oxygen, the first network owned by and operated for women.

Michealene met Gerry years ago at a small luncheon in Beverly Hills, California. She never forgot how impressed she was with how much Gerry valued loyalty. In fact, Gerry told her, "My father taught me: if you can't be loyal, you can't be anything. I believe that applies to everything: customers, companies, employees, family."

Throughout her career, Gerry continued to "walk the walk" and honor that wisdom passed down from her own father. Michealene remembers that when a colleague became embattled on an outside board, it was Gerry who rallied around her and said, "What she needs right now is for us to support her." As a result, this fellow female executive was able to survive and thrive through those daunting circumstances. Michealene says, "Whether it is a request to open a door for an internship or a chance to assist someone she may have not seen for many years, Gerry does it. Loyalty is a part of her DNA, and it is one of many reasons she is incredibly valued by those who count themselves among her friends."

Leaving the glamour of Hollywood and the excitement of Manhattan, our search for wise women continued to India. A former student of Deborah's told us our wise women tour wouldn't be complete without Kiran Bedi. She is so revered in Indian society that we were told when she walks the streets, large crowds of people gather to touch her or to hear her speak. His holiness the Dalai Lama launched a Web site in support of Kiran and wrote the foreword to her book *It's Always Possible*.

Recently voted India's most respected woman and a role model for one-sixth of the world's population, Kiran began her journey as India's first woman police officer. No stranger to controversy, Kiran was exiled to Asia's largest and most notorious prison, the New Delhi Tihar Jail. Kiran transformed the unruly hellhole into a global model for prison reform. Subsequently, Kofi Annan of the United Nations appointed Kiran to the International Policing System, making her the world's top cop.

Kiran's remarkable accomplishments might stem from her attitude. She says attitude is solidly entrenched and that we must be consciously aware of it at all times. She tells young women to be fearless and to realize that "nothing is permanent. What is permanent," Kiran says, "is your attitude to the moment. That is what is within your control."

During her career in a part of the world where women have always been second-class citizens, Kiran has been a lightning rod for as much controversy as praise. She says, "I live from match to match. Not to beat others but to challenge myself. I also don't back down from decisions that I think are legally, morally, and ethically right. The moral strength of the decision gives me courage."

Red Hot Mamas

You must dance like no one is watching, love like you have never been hurt, sing as if no one is listening, and live like it is heaven on earth. . . .
　—*Anonymous*

Our search for wise women led us to the discovery of a variety of grassroots groups that celebrate the sharing of women's wisdom. These groups exist all over the world. Take for example, Mary Reagan, the self-proclaimed Queen of the Red Hot Mamas in Santa Clara, California. She founded one of the fantastic groups we were fortunate enough to discover. Mary, at the age of eighty-three, gathers her clan of thirty to kick up their heels and hit the town. "When you get older," Mary says, "you find that women are your constants. Having women friends has saved my life so many times."

Whether Mary and her group are having high tea, a trip to the museum, or an afternoon at the horse races, the conversations are always rollicking good fun. Underneath the frivolity are also deeply satisfying discussions of everything from beloved pets to the lasting legacies left by loved ones. Mary and her Red Hot Mamas are just one example of how we can share common life experiences and face life together—while extending our hand to and holding the hands of other women.

Sassy Pink Peppers

Helping one another is part of the religion of our sisterhood.
—*Louisa May Alcott, writer (1832–1888)*

Terry Matheis didn't choose divorce. However, she did choose to keep her sense of humor and to seek out friendships with other single mothers and their children. Those connections proved so beneficial that Terry guessed other women would appreciate having an opportunity to participate in a similar group. So she founded the Sassy Pink Peppers, a nationwide community where single mothers, upon joining, are connected with fifty other single women in their local communities. Can you imagine? Instead of having to "go it alone," these fortunate women almost immediately have their own "paint dates" with women just like them who can share their collective wisdom, support, and en-courage-ment.

Whether from the click of a mouse, a telephone call, an e-mail or simply a chance or random meeting in your local Starbucks, wise women reside among us. Right now, today, make a promise to yourself to find the women of wisdom in your community. Ask them questions and listen closely to their answers. The lessons of wise women are priceless.

50. Apply these lessons learned.

Life should not be a journey to the grave with the intention of arriving safely in an attractive and well-preserved body, but rather to skid sideways, chocolate in one hand, Martini in the other, body thoroughly used up, totally worn out, and screaming, "Woo hoo—what a ride!"
—*Anonymous*

Lives We Didn't Order

So tell me, what is it you intend to do with your one precious life?
— Mary Oliver, poet (1935–   )

As we write these last words, the four of us will begin a new year. In looking back over our many years of friendship, we realize that we have all had "lives we didn't order." At times, we would have willingly traded our lives for what was behind Door Number Three. Yet, we can honestly say that we are wiser because of our life experiences. And we are richer—richer in spirit, in wisdom, and in joy.

During the years it took to write this book, our lives have continued to change. Deborah still believes in miracles because she lives with one every day—her husband. Mike continues to defy medical predictions, and we hope he will continue this journey for many years. Her son entered college this year, and her little girl, who used to run around the table shrieking and playing hide-and-seek with Jackie's daughter, will soon be entering high school. Deborah is writing another business book, and she continues to work with leaders in corporations and government. In the future, she would like to launch an international wise women's tour, going into communities around the globe, looking for the lessons of wise women and sharing their stories with the world.

Michealene had another baby, bringing the total to three boys under the age of nine. In her spare time, she managed to buy the rights to a number of scripts and books. She is busy raising funding to turn these stories into feature films which she plans to direct and produce. She is currently the spokesperson for Women's Independent Cinema, a San Francisco start-up that focuses on furthering women's storytelling. She and her husband recently bought and restored a 1926 historic house called Hummingbird Hill. In addition to three boys, they have two dogs, four lizards, sixteen chickens, and a host of wild animals that visit their home.

Jan and her husband Rob say that at last count their blended family is still standing—though in different parts of the world. One daughter is working in London; another just returned from studying in Australia. One is working for her dad and is doing well. One son returned to college and the other is looking at colleges with the cutest coeds! (Did we mention that when we started this book, all of her children were in elementary or high school?)

Jan is busy producing a new television show called Pacific Fusion and continues to consult for private companies in communications and media. In the future, she would love to place women into boardrooms and corporations. There is a name for this—they are called headhunters, and it sounds terrific to Jan.

Jackie was married during the writing of this book. We planned her wedding for her, down to the dress she was wearing and the food she would be serving. Her oldest son goes to college in the fall, and her youngest daughter will soon be entering middle school. She and her husband, Barry, have a cabin on a lake. Jackie took up fly-fishing—something none of us could imagine she would ever do. She loves the cabin in the woods and looks forward to every visit.

Jackie ran for lieutenant governor of the state of California but lost the primary race by a few percentage points. As we write this book, Jackie is contemplating her next career, and we are reminded that change and reinvention in a woman's life is a never-ending process. We look forward to watching what Jackie will do next.

Finding Your Own Path to Wisdom

Get wisdom!!
Wisdom is the principal thing;
And in all your getting, get understanding.
Exalt her, and she will promote you;
She will bring you honor, when you embrace her.
　　—Proverbs 4:5–9

We have shared fifty ways that our lives have benefited from knowing one another. We have also shared the collective wisdom of many
inspiring women who are examples of what we can do if we just take
the few steps required to begin. We hope you have enjoyed these
stories and suggestions. More important, we hope you are motivated
to follow up and apply them in your everyday life. Please take the
time to do the exercises in the WIT Kit sections. We know that in the
lives of busy women, the exercises can help you rise to the top even
when life keeps trying to drag you down. We are certain that we can't
control what happens in our lives, but we can go about creating the
quality of life we want now, not someday in the future.

　　Please join us on this journey. Contact us to share your stories,
your wisdom, and your insights. We'd love to feature your lessons
learned on our Web site, *www.thisisnotthelifeiordered.com.*

　　We'd welcome the opportunity to connect you with the other
wise women who can join you and support you. Until then, best
wishes in the pursuit of turning lives you may not have ordered into
ones you love immensely.

The WIT Kit
Exercises and Tools for Rebuilding Dreams and Finding Wisdom

Within your heart, keep one still, secret spot where dreams may go.
—Louise Driscoll, poet (1875–1957)

1. In your Wit Kit Journal make an entry of three big dreams you have—don't edit or critique—just write down your dreams. What aspect of your dreams can you build into your future right now? If you hope to write a book, can you begin to simply write a paragraph each day? If you wish to launch a business can you reach out to another business owner and get advice? Attend a trade show? Call the SCORE group—a volunteer group of seasoned executives who advise small business owners?

2. Can you identify a "dream catcher" in your life? The blue-haired lady was Deborah's dream catcher. She or he is the person who inspires you to follow your dreams. Start looking for that special dream catcher.

3. In your Wit Kit Journal make a list of the wisest women you know. Some you may know personally, others may be famous women you cull from the rich history of our world. What do you admire about these women? What are the qualities? When you think of them how do you feel? What can you learn from them? How can you launch your own version of the "wise women tour" in your community? Do you have friends who would join you in your search?

References

7. *Be willing to make great mistakes.*

The 'Oops Center,' *Exploration Research Journal*. Press release, Vanderbilt University, December 14, 2000.

Dr. Bjorn Olsen, Harvard University, founder of *Journal of Negative Results*. CBS Radio Network Interview with Charles Osgood, May 4, 2004.

11. *Don't wait until you are depressed or desperate (or both) to network.*

UCLA press release with summary and findings of UCLA Landmark Study on Friendship, featuring Laura Cousins Klein, PhD, June 2003.

13. *Move on, move up, or move out.*

Peggy Klaus, excerpts from speech, "Women and Leadership Summit," San Francisco, CA, June 2004.

16. *Realize that risks are part of the package.*

Laura Liswood, excerpt from Women's Leadership Project, Kennedy School of Government, Harvard University, June 1996.

20. *Walk through fields of fear.*

From Vornida Seng and excerpts from her interview with *People* magazine, May 2001.

25. *Know that courage isn't only owned by heroes.*

National Association of Women Business Owners, Silicon Valley Chapter Newsletter, June 2003.

26. *When you are short on dollars, be rich in spirit.*

National Center on Women and Aging, "Sitting Pretty or Sitting Duck," 1998 findings.

28. *Don't wait until your financial DNA has to be put on life support.*

AARP and Brandeis University Study on Women and Finance, April 2000.

34. *Recognize that chocolate melts in order to take a new form.* Adapted from articles written by Peter Fimrite for the *San Francisco Chronicle,* September 2005.

36. *Be grateful the dog did not pee on the carpet.*

Research and information provided to us by Dr. Robert Emmons, University of California, Davis, April 2004.

42. *Persist.*

Used with permission, Dr. Judith Orloff, Harmony Books; A Division of Random House, December 2005.

45. *Refuse to be imprisoned by your past.*

The International Resilience Project: Research and Application, Dr. Edith Grotberg. In *Proceedings of the 53rd Annual Convention of ICP: Cross-Cultural Encounters.* Emily Miao (Ed). Taipei, Taiwan: General Innovation Service, 1996.

47. *Seek a dream catcher.*

"Rules For Dreamers," Dr. Ivan Scheier. Excerpted from *The Grapevine Volunteer Newsletter,* Sacramento, CA, April 1996.

48. *Schedule a paint date.*

The Maslow Business Reader, Dr. Abraham Maslow and Deborah C. Stephens, New York: John Wiley and Sons, 1999.